KISSING THE FROGS

A Widow's Safari into the Online Dating Jungle

Lia Rose

First Edition

PAGE PUBLISHING, INC.
New York, NY

First originally published by Page Publishing, Inc. 2018

ISBN 978-1-64214-460-4 (Paperback)
ISBN 978-1-64214-461-1 (Digital)

Printed in the United States of America

Contents

Prologue Gianna Reigns Supreme! 5

537 Days: My First Stint Online

Chapter 1: The Profile..13

Chapter 2: Liar, Liar, Pants on Fire..23

Chapter 3: P.R.I.C.K..27

Chapter 4: Kissing Is an Art and Not Everyone Is a Van Gogh!...31

Chapter 5: My Little Black Book (aka My Purple Love Line Phone) 34

Chapter 6: The Firing Squad...37

Chapter 7: It's a Bird, It's a Plane, It's My Diaphragm!.................42

Chapter 8: Gravity's Downfall 45

Chapter 9: The Dent...51

Chapter 10: Hair Today, Gone Tomorrow.......................................53

Chapter 11: Please Read the Owner's Manual When Wielding Heavy Machinery.......................................56

Chapter 12: Casanova and the Chiropractor 64

Chapter 13: Norman! I've Hit Rock-Bottom..................................68

Chapter 14: By the Number...72

Chapter 15: Sweet Symphonic Sounds...75

Chapter 16: The Grand Delusion 79

Chapter 17: The One I Would Have Given My Heart To (aka Starbucks Guy)...82

Self-Discovery Chapters
Chapter 18: You Can't Get Everything at Walmart........................89
Chapter 19: Reading between the Lines: Online Dating at a Glance..93
Chapter 20: Clean-Up on Aisle 3! 101
Chapter 21: Oh, My Goddess! 105

Take Two: Second Time around, a Glutton for Punishment
Chapter 22: Groundhog Day 111
Chapter 23: Talked Off the Ledge and an Epic Limerick 116
Chapter 24: But Seriously, Folks...120
Chapter 25: The Movie Ending 129
Chapter 26: The Tree Frog 133
Chapter 27: My Stroke of Luck..139

Prologue

Gianna Reigns Supreme!

This book is a comedy because life is funny as hell no matter what is going on. It's how you look at it. So though it was not my intention to write a prologue, it will help to explain a little of the back story.

"A *nice* Catholic, Italian girl wouldn't do that, you know!" I heard it often, but not from my parents or family members as you might suspect, but from Shelly. Who is Shelly, you might ask? Shelly was my inner voice for the first forty-eight years of my life. She had dark-brown hair (which I believe *is* my natural color), and she was always wearing a white holy communion dress and veil covered in lace with white tights and white patent leather shoes (which she tapped incessantly) and pretty lace gloves. Her voice was sweet one moment and demanding the next, and she reminded me of Angelica on *Rugrats*, a show my children watched ad nauseam when they were children. She kept me on the straight and narrow my whole life with that one little phrase. Every now and again, she would interject gems like, "You're the oldest, so you have to set an example for your younger siblings," or "Mom and Dad will be very disappointed in you."

I was the model daughter, the dutiful oldest sibling, the steadfast wife, and the loving and caring mother. Don't get me wrong, I loved and gladly lived each one of these titles. I had wonderful parents that loved and supported me. I loved being a part of a large happy family. And when I married my soul mate and had my own children, it was beyond my wildest dreams, but to this day, I don't know if some of the choices I made were my own, or if I made them out of a sense of fear or duty. All I remember was Shelly repeating her mantras and me obeying her every word. I remember being afraid of so many things, and because I was the "artsy-fartsy" one in the family, and was sensitive, sometimes to the point of tears, I was looked upon by my brothers and sisters as the weak one. My parents, on the other hand, though they were strictest with me, told me only about fifteen years ago that they felt I was the strongest because I was able to adapt to any situation. My mother had always said, "When you need to be strong, you will be." I didn't believe her until 2001.

November 11, 2001, two months after the world was shaken by the tragic events of 9-11, my world was shaken by the news that my thirty-seven-year-old husband, Dennis, had colon cancer. From that point on, through doctors' visits, tests, second opinions, treatments, surgeries, taking care of my three young sons, it was a whirlwind of activities.

Through it all, I heard Shelly, patronizing at times, telling me, "For better for worse, in sickness and in health, or you are the dutiful wife and mother. Everyone is depending on you, and you aren't allowed to crumble. It's not the right thing to do." I was resentful of her, reminding me of things I already knew. It was then I started to feel and hear another voice. It was hard to hear her over the din of Shelly's constant yapping and tapping, but the day we received the news about Dennis, I heard this voice say, "That *really* sucks, but get your ass up off the ground. You are strong, and you can do this!"

I felt empowered for a fleeting moment. Through the nine-year rollercoaster ride which was my husband's battle with cancer, there were times when I felt like running away, and Shelly would be there, tapping that damn little white patent leather shoe of hers, pointing me back. Every now and then, I would hear a voice that said, "Do something for yourself. Take a bath, go watch one of your favorite movies, remove yourself from the situation for a while." And one time, when Shelly was contemplating our next goodie two-shoes maneuver, I learned the name of this new voice was Gianna.

I had become a warrior, embattled and bruised sometimes but steadfast and strong most times, and Gianna, my inner voice, had helped me. Gianna was beautiful, confident, strong, playful, and funny—everything I am inside. Every once in a while, Gianna would lock Shelly out of the house or body slam her out of the way when she was about to speak or tap. I found it amusing and a welcome change.

In May 2010, Dennis went into the hospital. This had happened a few times before, so when we were just waiting there for hours, Dennis sent me home to get some rest. This was the only time in my husband's nine-year battle that he had asked me, "Rose, what if I can't do this anymore?" With a heavy heart, I responded, "Then I'm going to have to be brave."

On the way home, I got a call that he had taken a drastic turn and was in the ICU. It was as if he needed my permission. He needed to know I could be brave. Shelly stepped right in front of the car at that moment, and it came to a screeching stop. Was this frightened little girl always going to be who I was? I think *not*!

Gianna came at Shelly with such ferocity that it created a fire storm. There was hair pulling and bitch slapping, screaming, and crying. At one point, I saw Shelly take off her little white gloves and smack Gianna across the face, challenging her to a duel. This confrontation looked like a cross between *The Matrix* fight scenes and the lightsaber duel in *Star Wars*. Sometimes it looked like something out of a Three Stooges movie, but in the end, Gianna reigned supreme, and I no longer felt or heard from Shelly again. I was no longer that pristine, frightened little girl in the white communion dress, and I had Gianna, my inner strength, to thank for it.

I called my children at school and told them I was going to pick them up. I called my entire family and Dennis' family to tell them of the developments. I brought Dennis's grandmother with us to the hospital. I knew what I had to do, and I was doing it! I was talking to doctors, social workers, hospice nurses. I was trying to do what I knew Dennis would want me to do. And I knew he would want me to be brave.

We transferred him to a wonderful hospice unit, and family began to come in from out of state. At first, we were packed into a very small room, and Dennis was on high doses of oxygen and was in a semicomatose state and heavily medicated. The doctors' were grim about Dennis's prognosis, but in usual Dennis fashion, he rallied once again, and there were plans to get him home. I was tired and had spent many nights at the hospital listening to my brave husband fighting to breathe. When he would finally fell asleep, his breathing would relax a little, and I would walk the halls of the hospice unit with Gianna at my side. This place was strangely peaceful; no beeping machines, only nurses that were amazingly friendly and supportive, which gave me time to think, to pray, to cherish every moment.

Gianna reassured me that I could do anything I set my mind to, so I rallied the troops at home, and we prepared to get Dennis home. We took my office, which was on the first floor, right off the hub of the house, my kitchen and made it into a bedroom. We threw things in boxes, took apart my huge desk and threw it onto the front lawn, hung some pictures, got a nice soft lamp and tried to make the room look homey. I had some wonderful friends and family to help me.

After restructuring my first floor, meeting with doctors, nurses, and social workers, we got Dennis home around 4:30 p.m. on a Friday afternoon. Dennis was happy to be home, but the troubled look on his face never left him. He struggled to breathe and never felt like he was getting enough oxygen. He didn't speak because it was taking too much energy and oxygen to do so, so he was writing things down on a pad of paper.

His writing became more frenzied by about 7:00 p.m., and when we had a brief power outage, he went into a complete panic. It was his worst fear realized. We had to call 911 and get him back to the hospital. Dennis didn't want to die at home. He didn't want his death to be our memory of him in the house. Paramedics, EMTs, firemen, and family filled this eleven by eleven foot room, and finally, Dennis wrote that extra people had to leave. I had to have our boys come in to say their goodbyes, just in case something happened on the way to the hospital.

We managed to get him to the hospital. In the hospital room, the nurse asked my husband, "Dennis, how are you doing?"

In typical fashion, he said, "Fine."

That was the last word I ever heard my husband utter. From that point on, it was comfort measures only. They gave him morphine to help with the breathing and to help him relax, but this also meant that he was almost in a comatose state.

We all stayed by this side the entire night, commandeering every cot, recliner, or chair that was available on the hospice unit. We talked to him, played seventies music in the background as the nurses came in to periodically give us an update.

My husband battled cancer for nine years, and my youngest was only six when he was diagnosed, so that's all he really knew, but Dennis had rallied so many times that as I watched my son, I don't think he believed his father would really die. I felt the same way. I never stopped believing and hoping we would get a miracle.

At 3:36 p.m., my husband opened his eyes, he looked around at each one of us during a '70s song called "Beach Baby," then took his last breath, which was as ferocious as a lion's roar. He didn't want to leave. He was pissed that the cancer had gotten him.

At that moment, my heart broke instantly into shards of broken glass, but nothing compared to the pain my heart felt as I looked up into the faces of my children. Their hearts broke before my eyes, and I was powerless to do anything about it. In the hospice unit, they hang an iridescent blue light on the door, and they ring a chime to acknowledge that someone has passed. Had Shelly still been around at this point, I feel sure that I would have lapsed into that scared child mode again. Not that I wasn't scared, I was petrified, but I wasn't a child. I was strong, and as I walked out of the hospital with the little blue light, I felt Gianna and I heard her say, "I'm proud of you, and you can do this. You are a strong woman!"

537 Days:
My First Stint Online

Chapter 1

The Profile

(Insert *Dragnet* theme song here. Google it if you have to, and imagine a man's deep voice reading the following paragraph.)

Bum, ba-dump, bum.

The story you are about to hear is true. The names have been changed to protect the "idiots!"

Bum, ba-dump, bump, bump

This is Rose D'Alisio, widowed at forty-eight after twenty-one years of marriage, forced to embark on a dangerous safari to complete immersion into another world—the dangerous jungle of online dating. This is her story. (Insert obscure *Law and Order* sound here.)

Please excuse the stage directions, but as my life often times resembles the fiasco, drama, and pageantry of a Broadway extravaganza, and the fact that I have directed community theater shows since 1990, added with the fact that I have been teaching high school theater arts for fourteen years, I almost write everything as if I were writing a script, especially e-mails. You can't hear the tone of an e-mail, so I always add stage directions. Soundtracks and special effects, props and staging, costumes, hairstyles and makeup, actors and divas, I've dealt with them all. But nothing, and I mean nothing, in my life could have prepared me for the mind-numbing, ego-thrashing thrill ride that is online dating. (I dislike thrill rides, by the way.)

My story is true and not sugarcoated, though you will notice periods where I lapse into goody two-shoes mode when describing certain things, usually involving sex. Old habits die hard. Picture, if you will, a woman (me) arriving in Africa for an adventurous safari wearing nothing but a sundress (it's going to be hot), high-heeled stiletto sandals (they go with the dress after all) and a beaded purse (the one that looks pretty but isn't even big enough to hold my phone when I go out, so I have to stick the phone in my bra), and that's how prepared I was to attempt online dating, or dating in general, after my husband died. (My friends would not be the least bit surprised, however, if that is how I really did show up for a safari adventure.)

After my husband died, I was anxious about a lot of things, but most especially that I would never be looked at as a woman again. I'd be labeled as the sad widow, and I would be alone and lonely the rest of my life. This led me to test the waters of online dating before I was ready to because in my mind, if I found someone right away, I wouldn't have to feel the pain of my splintered and broken heart. Wrong! You can run and you can hide, but in the end, you have to feel every pain in order to move on and heal.

With my newfound inner strength and a newfound inner voice, I made an attempt to move on as a forty-eight-year-old woman who was too young to be old and too old to be young. I was back out in the dating world, a world that I wasn't too thrilled about being out in the first time around, and now I was almost thirty years older. But surely it couldn't be *that* different than it was the first time, right?

One of the first challenges that faced me when I started my online dating adventure was to write a proper profile. This proved to be more difficult than it would seem; not only did I have to give a sense of the person I was but I also had to give a sense of the person I was looking for. After pacing back and forth virtually in my mind for about an hour, complaining out loud many times that I hate talking about myself, Gianna suggested that I start with what I want in a man, and then she would proof it for me.

I had seen those personals ads long before online dating in rag mags, and I always wondered who was desperate enough to put an ad in a newspaper for a mate. DWF, SWF, WWF, GWM, etc., and the words that followed *looking for* usually curled my communion white toes. And here I was, telling the world what I was looking for. My transition relationship after my husband died had taught me a lot about what I did and didn't want. The number one thing that was important to me was honesty, so I proceeded to be honest.

Widowed white female, fifty, who is horny as hell *at the moment*, looking for a tall, dark, handsome man with a great bod, who is hung like a horse and knows how to ride me like a well-trained equestrian. Gianna (my inner voice) had just taken a bite of a cannoli (she can eat anything and never gain an ounce, which makes me sick) and started to choke as I read aloud my first line.

"You can't write that!" she exclaimed after I gave her a quick Heimlich maneuver and she started breathing again.

"Why not, I'm just being honest!" I said. She put up her hand while she continued to cough and clear her throat, but then let me continue.

Widowed white female, fifty, who is horny as hell, looking for a tall, dark, handsome man with a great bod who is hung like a horse and knows how to ride me like a well-trained equestrian. He should know how to cook and clean and especially do laundry. Being handy around the house is a must. He should be loyal, faithful (only have eyes for me), trustworthy, and treat me like a queen. No sports couch potatoes please. He should know how to dance tango like Antonio Banderas in the movie *Take the Lead*, kiss like Patrick Swayze in *Dirty Dancing*, sing love song duets with me like Ewan McGregor in *Moulin Rouge*, and make me laugh like Mel Brooks (any movie take your pick). Oh yeah, and he should have a job. I'm 100% Italian, so I love hard, cook great, but don't piss me off because I'm going to let you hear about it.

I looked up from my computer for a moment to see Gianna reaching for another cannoli. "If you are going to do us in, I might as well choke on another cannoli and die happy," she said snidely. Then she started sputtering in Italian again. "*Donna dissoluta!*" I usually didn't understand a word she said in Italian, but I understood that one. What I wasn't expecting was the flying cannoli that was coming projectile toward my head. "You just can't write that! Every guy is proud of his Mr. Johnson and feels that he is hung like a horse. And the only line the guys will see is the one about riding you like a well-trained equestrian. You are going to get every loser, Tom, Dick, or Harry—no pun intended."

In reality, I never would have posted anything like this. I was afraid of rejection. My husband was the only man I had ever been with in *that* way, and I waited until marriage even for that. And he was sick for so long and unable to be intimate because of the radiation, chemotherapy, and without going into detail, things that had been affected by his initial surgery. So my seeming infatuation with sex was a merely a smoke screen to keep me from writing what I wanted to write. "Love me. Pick me up and hold me until my heart heals. Please be my everything. Make me smile and laugh and please don't hurt me."

"Help me write it then!" I snapped back to Gianna with ricotta cheese dribbling down my face from the cannoli. Gianna appeared in her business attire—pencil skirt, high heels, and glasses—looking very professional when she sat down at my computer. "Let's leave the widow part out of the profile because you already mention it above in your marital status, and that's not all that you are about, and we don't want the guys to get the whole 'living up to the dead husband' hang up. Write this."

> I am a curvy, sassy, funny, creative, and passionate woman who is excited to start a new phase of my life. I love to laugh and love to make others laugh, and I love to dance. I am looking for a confident, passionate, independent, honest, sexy man who enjoys being romantic and knows how to treat a woman like a lady. Hopefully we can share mutual interests, exciting outings, and also romantic evenings at home, discovering what makes each other tick. Must be a great kisser (deal breaker).

I settled on this watered-down version of my profile, adding blurbs about walks on the beach, sunsets, nights by the fire, which are things that I truly love, but I didn't realize that every profile lists these things, and they become very clichéd and boring.

Being a newbie to the dating scene, my first profile garnered me quite a few winks, pokes, and e-mails. My first reaction was, "That was easy!" Then it very quickly became work; taking compatibility quizzes, taking flattering pictures with only an arm's length difference, answering e-mails, instant messages, and texts.

To keep your profile visible and highlighted, the sites suggested that you keep your profile current and change it often. It didn't take me long to discover that even if you changed one word in the profile, it bumped your profile up and informed all the would-be suitors that you had updated your profile. It also didn't take me long to discover that there are certain words you shouldn't use in your profile, like sexy, because then would-be suitors can search for key words, and sexy means *sex* to them, of course, so does toilet paper, scotch tape, and pumpkins. They are men after all.

My second profile (which means I didn't get my prince right out of the gate) read like follows:

> I am a strong, sexy, smart, creative, funny, and passionate woman who is finally confident and comfortable in her own skin. There is an incredible freedom in that. I am ready and willing to start this new phase of my life, but you have to start out small (dates, chats, friendship, etc.).
>
> I have curves gentlemen. I have never been nor will ever be a size zero. Zero means naught, nothing, and perhaps someone should have taught these poor ladies to eat like normal people. Call me a Renaissance woman. Leonardo Da Vinci and Raphael might have found me an exquisite model for their paintings. LOL. I am always trying to better myself for myself, not for anyone

> else. I exercise regularly, swim, walk, do strength training, meditate daily, but I especially love to *dance.*
>
> I want a relationship (there, I said it!) *eventually*, but it would be great to just go out and meet people; date, have fun, etc. I'm looking for a friend, confidant, a partner in crime, a lover, and all the wonderful things that go along with having that wonderful connection with one person.
>
> My man: I would like a funny, smart, sexy, passionate, trustworthy, exciting, romantic man. Did I mention funny? And it would be great if you were a gentleman and knew how to treat a lady. And I'd like you to follow the rules of a good golf swing—*follow through*. In other words, please say what you mean and *mean* what you say. Oh, BTW, gotta be a great kisser (deal breaker).
>
> Are you out there?

Over the course of my adventure through the online dating jungle, I changed my profile multiple times. On the opening day of fishing, I changed it to fishing terms like "Angler wanted," "good catch," and "reel me in". Around Super Bowl Time, I spent two hours researching football terms that I brilliantly composed into a witty comparison to dating like "touchdowns," "illegal pass," "don't fumble the ball," etc. I thought I was really quite clever.

And of course, around the time of the Daytona 500 and NASCAR season, I was asking the gentlemen "to start their engines" or maybe it was start my engines . . . I don't know.

I quickly discovered that men don't want to read a novel in your profile. *If* you can even get them to read your profile at all! I calculated that I had three sentences to grab their attention because three sentences did not require the user to scroll down the page to read more.

I tried humor. My opening line was a quote I found online, "If a man remembers the color of your eyes after a first date, chances are, you have small boobs." I got many responses and chuckles but no dates.

My shortest profile was four words: Looking for *a man*.

That's when they matched me to a transgender person named SissyWilly whose profile described him as a "Man looking for a woman who wants a man to dress like a woman and be a wild woman in the bedroom." *What?* This is absolutely true. I have his profile and picture in my research.

And my last profile before I left the dating sites completely (the first time) read as follows:

> This is it, gentlemen. My subscription expires on August 21, and I'm not renewing. So if you are a "handsome prince" waiting for the right moment to swoop in on your white horse and rescue me from the dastardly clutches of the Online Dating Monster, now might be the time.

Along my perilous journey, I have encountered numerous scribes (guys who want to be pen pals), a host of gremlins (start out nice, then send pictures of their . . . lances), and a myriad of trolls (scammers, phone sexers, and guys that make dates and don't show up.) But alas, there have been a few nice men, and I do know of tales of love, so I'm not saying there hasn't been happily ever after for people I have known.

In my profiles, I have tried to be serious, funny, and sarcastic. I have used sports, NASCAR, and fishing analogies to no avail. But every word of *my* profile is true, and that is all I am asking for in a man: truthfulness and *chemistry*.

After a few dates (which I will describe in later chapters), my subscription ended without even a whimper, and I vowed never to do online dating again.

I would be remiss if I didn't include some of the profiles that I weeded through with a machete while on my safari. These are actual and uncensored profiles. I did not edit them in any way, and my only wish is that I could show you the pictures that accompanied them so you could get a visual.

1. College entrepreneur

   Since of humor will spoil you love dogs pretty lade back like to drive like cars all around good human and I do maintance for houses and apartments not filthy rich but I get by comfertabley.

2. In his own words

   Hi ladies i have many intress just a few are dining movies the country rides the outdoors nice walks together walking in the warm rain can be fun i love the outdoors walking in the crisp air. I am look for a woman who takes pride in her appearance is somewhat in shape. But you know what ladies bieng with the one you want to be with is the best nothing tops that i wish every one the best on here. I love the outdoors

I'm not sure what colleges they attended, but they must have been a new age college where they didn't require their students to fit into pesky molds and stereotypes, and they didn't have to adhere to conventions like being able to spell, capitalize letters or use lowercase letters, and use punctuation.

And most of the profiles I read were like the following—seemingly normal, fine upstanding men. This type of man always had very flattering pictures of themselves and often seemed like they would be pictured on *Golf Digest*, *GQ*, or some other classy magazine. This taught me to read between the lines, but as you will find out, sometimes you just can't get a feel for someone until you talk to them or meet them. The profile below is for a gentleman with a huge foot fetish, and all he wanted was pictures of my feet in various shoes and for me to tell him in graphic detail about my latest pedicure

> 45 y/o DWM 5'10" Dark Blonde, Blue Eyes, Athletic and Toned, Technical Computers
>
> I would describe myself as honest, hardworking, reliable, and caring. I enjoy the outdoors, baseball games, bicycling, beaches, hiking. I'm a professional who works in the IT field and enjoys his job. I enjoy a healthy lifestyle that includes a few days a week in the gym. I am financially/emotionally/physical fit. I enjoy being with women who are happy, intelligent, witty, and enjoy the life they have.
>
> She should be confident, open, and loves life. I find chemistry between two people to be an important factor in relationships and to find it in you. I am looking for a woman who wants to have fun and enjoy being with a man who will appreciates her for who she is. Things are clicking well. I would like to meet some really interesting people that fit well; people that enjoy life and stay apart from negativity.
>
> Meeting some place for coffee/drink, then going for a walk and spend time asking each other questions . . . discovering each other's interests, hobbies, get to know each other.

And when they say that a picture's worth a thousand words, it's true. The first time I did a search within the site, even before I became a member, my search criteria was as follows: men, forty to sixty, within fifty miles of my home, *no smoking*, casual drinking.

I wasn't specific about personal appearance but put in some of the choices the site gave me like: slim, a few extra pounds, average, athletic, and toned (because who wouldn't want athletic and toned?). I was specific that they had to be single, divorced, or widowed because I would not date someone who was only separated.

The first list of "the chosen" looked like wanted posters in the post office. I was devastated! There were hundreds upon hundreds of faces, and most of them resembled movie villains or cartoon characters.

One of the men on the list had long curly hair but was bald on top and closely resembled Larry from the Three Stooges. He touted himself as a geek who didn't like technology. Another man had taken a picture so close to the mirror that every pore, pock mark, and nose hair on his face was visible, and the distortion made his nose look like Jimmy Durante's.

And one gentlemen, who was fifty years old, had long brown hair (mind you, I love long hair on guys, so I wasn't complaining about the hair), a seventies Tom Selleck mustache, and he was wearing black jeans, a black shirt, platform-type shoes, and a gigantic gothic cross around his neck. I had to actually click on his profile to see the rest of it. Evidently, he was a huge, and I mean *huge*, Kiss fan. The remaining pictures were of him at the Kiss museum in Las Vegas, where he must have been allowed to try on Kiss costumes, including full Gene Simmons Demon Destroyer boots. There were pictures of him dressed as Kiss, in a bedroom with Kiss posters, which I suspect was in his mother's basement.

All these men could have been very nice people, and beauty is only skin deep, but there has to be an attraction, and we haven't even got to the matches yet. So please read on!

Chapter 2

Liar, Liar, Pants on Fire

One day, one of my Facebook friends posted a meme that read, "How much better would life be if a liar's pants really did catch on fire?" My comment to this meme was simple: "It sure would make online dating a lot easier!" Even on the phone, if you had that option, you could ask your respective date a question, and if he screamed in pain, you'd know he was lying to you. When you actually got so far as to be asked on a date, it might be somewhat amusing to see him run out of the restaurant screaming toward the nearest horse trough conveniently located outside the restaurant to put out his flaming ass!

Recently, I was discussing online dating with a bunch of friends while we were relaxing at the beach. A guy friend asked me, "So tell me, Rose, did you lie on your profile?" And I said, "Absolutely not!" And this was absolutely true. (If they had asked my weight, I would have lied because it's none of their damn business!) I had current pictures, my age was right, and everything I put in the profile was the truth, and not some watered down version of it either. I found out very quickly, however, that lying was the norm in the online dating world. It seemed most of the Adonis's on the site made $150,000 plus salaries, and they were all handsome, athletic, and toned entrepreneurs. (Note: Nowhere on the profile application does it ask about having teeth, but I will get into that in another chapter.)

Because the flaming pants thing isn't an option, I have had to become quite the sleuth. Thankfully, I have watched every crime drama known to man, including every *Matlock* and *Murder, She Wrote* episode, so I've gathered a myriad of valuable information for my online dating experience. For instance, when the scary music plays in the background, someone is going to die. If Mrs. Fletcher comes to visit you, no matter what city or state you live in, you are probably going to die. Never be the shortest, ugliest, or bespectacled person in a crowd of tall, tanned, blonde bimbos because even though one of them is probably going to die, you are going to die first. But I digress. These shows taught me the value of simple research, watching body language, listening to voice inflections, the powers of observation, and that a good hotdog hits the spot every once in a while. (Thanks, *Matlock*.)

It's actually quite scary when you think about it. You put yourself out there online, then talk, then meet. It really is worth finding out at least some information. So even at the earliest stages, I would try to find out as much information as possible. I liked a man who would get involved in a Twenty Questions type of banter—you know, favorites, etc. The hardest part most times was getting his last name. Once I had that, it was a lot easier to find or at least confirm some of the information he gave me.

In the beginning, I tried to join one of those people search sites, but the truth of the matter is that whatever rate you pay to join, you have to pay more to get the full report that has all the important information on it. The information they give you without paying more is simply available to almost everyone for free.

I follow these steps, which I call my "self-preservation tips available and largely known" (STALK for short). A girl can't be too careful, you know, and this is all information that is available on the good old worldwide web.

Google

I google his name in the web search and images. This may help confirm if he is telling you the truth about his name, his job, and other basics. If someone acts a little weird or his profile is too good to be true, I will google the text of his profile. Often times, scammers will use the same basic profile but will change the pictures or some of the vital statistics. I have actually used this search technique and discovered numerous hits and warnings on dating website scams.

Jud.ct.gov

This is a great resource for a number of things. One of the first things I check is if a guy is truly divorced. I have had dealings with guys that say they are divorced and are not. I have had guys say they are divorced when they are only separated and then have gone back to their wives two weeks before the divorce was to be final. (I won't date anyone who is just separated.) Once I checked out a potential date who had a litany of red flags listed on his divorce court proceedings, like restraining orders and custody battles, etc. You don't learn the whole story, but it might give you some indication of the baggage that this person carries. It will also let you search to see if there are any criminal or civil cases against him. This is not always perfect because you usually can search convictions and pending cases, but it doesn't always give you arrest warrants or cases that were dropped after they completed counseling or other state mandated rehabilitation.

Sex Offender Registry

Thankfully, none of my potential dates have appeared on the sex offender registry. That is, *if* they had actually given me their *real* name. It's actually kind of a nail-biting experience because the thought that there could be sex offenders on dating sites or anywhere actually is unnerving. But it gives you some valuable information and at least offers some consolation if he is not listed there. The drawbacks are that sex offenders have to register and give changes of address, and sometimes these fine, upstanding citizens don't do their civic duty.

Facebook

If they have a Facebook page, and it is public, it helps to see if they are telling the truth about their family or have offensive posts, extremist political rants, or other things that might be a rule breaker in your book (e.g., asking their friends to like *Polygamist Weekly* or *Mama's Boy Magazine*) It is just as appropriate to creep on their page as it is for employers to do it, and I know that is widely done. Their posts give a pretty good indication of their likes and their personality, good and bad. Hopefully you would have at least gotten him to do the Twenty Questions game with you, and his answers were very forthcoming.

I'm not a pessimist. In fact, I'm very much an optimist. And though I wish the world were a perfectly safe place and precautions weren't necessary, I'm afraid it is not, and you have to be careful. At some point in time, in any relationship, you have to take that leap of faith, but maybe if you do a little research ahead of time, at least you are jumping off that cliff with a bungee cord and some safety gear attached.

Chapter 3

P.R.I.C.K

Back in the olden days, messages were sent via Pony Express, smoke signals, bangs on a drum, homing pigeon, or raven. Harry Potter received messages by owl. But in a world where technology can pinpoint your exact location via GPS, you can reach someone on the opposite ends of the world by texting and hitting the send button, there are cameras on every phone, in every store, and on every corner, there is no excuse to stand someone up. *None!*

I have closed myself between two elevator doors while getting off at the wrong floor because I was distracted by a cute guy in the elevator. I have slipped across the deli floor and fallen in clogs while holding a five-foot long salami, which I did not drop. And I have fallen down in the middle of the busiest four-way intersection on Main Street during rush hour, holding six shopping bags, while falling out of my shoes—again clogs (damn, clogs!). But nothing is more humiliating than being stood up on a date. *Nothing!* In the movies, when you see that lonely-hearts person sitting there, there always seems to be a handsome prince or a fairy godmother there to save the day. This only happens in the movies, folks!

Very early on in the dating process, I was being pursued electronically (I know, sounds gross) by PurpleDurple32. He winked, I winked. He e-mailed, I e-mailed. He phoned, I picked up the phone. He asked to meet, I said yes, and we arranged the meeting at one of the local diners for a cup of coffee. I went into the restaurant and was seated at a seat near the window. Then I waited and waited and waited. At one point, I saw a car drive in and pull in a parking space, and from what I could see through the tinted windows of the car and the tinted windows of the diner, it was him. He sat for a few minutes, then left.

The waitress came over and asked if I was okay because I had made the mistake of telling her I was expecting someone. I wasn't okay. I was paralyzed. I couldn't move. *How do I get myself out of this restaurant without someone seeing the gigantic L for loser flashing neon green over my head?* I thought to myself. I had *never* been stood up before. To make matters worse, I had told my boys that I was going on a date, and my process was to keep the prospective date's profile and any contact information up on my computer "just in case."

I walked into my house, and my sons didn't even know what to say. One of them finally said, "Home so soon?" and I had to say the words I have never spoken in my life: "I got stood up."

Feeling dejected, I sat down at my computer and took this Romeo's profile and added it to the blocked profile section, which is your only, far be it from satisfying, recourse in the online dating world other than reporting him for lewd behavior. And being a jerk isn't really lewd behavior. There should really be an explosion button that you can push after a bad date where you can see an animation of his head exploding (just sayin'). He didn't call, he didn't text to say he wasn't coming. I was thinking to myself, car broke down? He could have called. He had a change of heart? He could have texted. He died? No such luck because I saw him active on the site later that evening.

I wish I could report that this never happened to me again, but alas that is not true. It happened many more times; different guys, different professions, all after I had conversed with them, or chatted online. I had Tiger49, who didn't "remember" that he made a date with me to get a cup of coffee, even though we texted each other, then tried to ask me out again and was surprised when I said, "No, you stood me up the last time."

Then there was HectorGiavanni, an Italian art dealer from California, who was being relocated to Connecticut, so he said. He made a date with me to meet at one of my favorite little restaurants on the lake for a cup of coffee or a drink. I went into the restaurant and got a table for two. I sat there looking out over the lake, getting sicker and sicker to my stomach with each second that ticked by, and I tried on numerous occasions to convince the waitress (really myself) that he was coming, he must have hit traffic, etc.

After the clock ticked 2700 times with no call (forty-five minutes to normal people that aren't sitting in a restaurant waiting for a date, paralyzed with dread about taking the walk of shame with the flashing loser sign above their head), I mustered the energy to walk out to my car. I texted him, with the intent of giving him a "what for" (which is old fashion speak for a WTF call), and he apologized, saying he was on a plane because he had to take an unexpected flight back to California for business. He said he was sorry and asked if we could try it again, the next time he was in town. He apologized after all, so that surely must negate all the humiliation, nausea, and shame I felt at the restaurant. I declined. Was he home laughing at me? Was he in the restaurant watching it play out? What joy did he get from it?

The last guy that did this to me, Batman4u, was awarded the POTY prize (pronounce *potty*), which is the prestigious distinction I awarded for being the biggest *prick of the year*. I don't mean to be crass, but sometimes you have to call a spade a spade.

For a week, we chatted online, talked on the phone, and finally, he asked me to meet him at a local bagel place for a cup of coffee. He was handsome, funny, well-spoken, had a good job, was self-sufficient, had one twelve-year-old daughter and ironically lived in the same town as I did.

It was eight o'clock on a beautiful sunny Sunday summer morning, and I decided to dress in a casual sundress and drive my '92 Miata to the date. I was feeling good about this one. I parked about ten spaces from the bagel place because I wasn't sure if there were available spaces farther down. I saw a man sitting at one of the outside tables under the umbrella who I thought resembled him from a distance. I walked towards him, levitated by the butterflies in my stomach. When I was about twenty feet away, he casually got up with his coffee, walked to his truck, got in, backed up, waited until I was within eye shot as he looked through the back window of his truck, then drove away.

I was nauseous; actually nauseous. No one ever died by sitting through a ten-minute cup of coffee with someone. *No one!* I could feel my heart beating in every pulse point in my body. I actually had to sit down at one of the outside tables to get my bearings. No one knew what had just transpired, but when a nice couple and their two young children came and sat down next to me and said, "Good Morning," I just blurted out, "I just got stood up on a date." They were sympathetic and kind, but once again, and this time because of my own doing, I had to take the walk of shame with my bright neon green, flashing loser sign following me and drive away in a bright yellow Miata. Priceless.

He didn't call, he didn't text. No apology came. This time, however, in addition to blocking this SOB, I sent him a text and an e-mail with various creative expletives and my hopes that his daughter never had to experience a prick like him when she started dating. But you all know how karma works.

Lessons Learned

- Never agree to meet for a date *inside* a restaurant; meet in the parking lot as long as it's safe. It will save you loads of humiliation
- Find out what kind of car he drives, then park directly behind him even if you have to double park or park illegally; this insures that he can sit through a ten-minute cup of coffee. A potential ten-dollar parking ticket is still better than the humiliation of being stood up.
- Don't blurt out to the world what you think the entire world knows but really doesn't know or care.
- Humiliation won't actually kill you, no matter how much it feels like it will.
- And I don't *drink coffee*, so why the hell do I keep meeting people for coffee?

Chapter 4

Kissing Is an Art and Not Everyone Is a Van Gogh!

I love kissing! *I love it!* This is how I like to be kissed. I call it the *leading-man kiss.* If it's a first kiss (with good chemistry), I like to feel the energy drawing our lips together before they actually touch. There needs to be a tease; lips touching with an air of mystery that approaches confidently but cautiously. There should be a wanting; a driving curiosity to enter the forbidden door, but a patience to not burst through it like an unwelcomed adversary at the door of a castle. Knock. Let me answer demurely. Our lips should always touch first and melt into a movement, like a gentle dance at first until we get our rhythm. Then the dance can become more passionate as we become more in sync with each other. Touch my face. If you really want to drive me wild, gently grasp my face near the nape of my neck. If I'm feeling playful, I might gently bite your lip, but it is important to wait—wait for the invitation. Then, and only then, should you venture through the door to the other side. Translation for the opposite sex: don't jam your tongue into my mouth right out of the gate. It's a huge turn off for me.

Finding a good kisser among all these online and even offline frogs was a dauntless task. I experienced Mushy Droolers, Torpedo Tonguers, Fish Lippers, or the ever-popular Flubber Lips (say that ten times fast).

Mushy Droolers seem to produce an exorbitant amount of drool. I can usually spot this phenomenon when he is speaking to me during the conversation part of our meeting; when he is not only regaling you with funny anecdotes or fascinating stories but he is also showering me with copious amounts of saliva. I always think to myself, *Man, I already took a shower tonight, and I got to use my yummy-smelling almond and honey scrub.* And I daydream for a second and . . . okay, I'm back. In the few instances when I have in fact let the "drooler" in for a kiss, he has come at me with mouth fully open, enveloping my tiny mouth, and leaving me with an unpleasant "ah, yes, you had the garlic bread with dinner" pool of saliva in my mouth. Now I fully realize that when you try to kiss someone passionately that there is going to be some spit swapping, but no one should leave an unwanted puddle behind. This type of kisser, and I had a few, also seems to be as excitable as a puppy as he slobbers me with kisses. And all I can say to him is, "Down, boy!"

Torpedo Tonguers—this category is pretty self-explanatory. There is nothing unobvious about these men. If I give him any indication that a kiss is imminent (which in the world of men could be as simple as dropping my napkin or asking where the ladies room is), he will purse his lips and stick that wet pointy thing right out at me, and I can see it coming from a mile away. Don't these men watch movies? TV? Hasn't he ever viewed a romantic kiss from a handsome leading man? Unless you are in a Will Ferrell comedy or something, why would you ever come at someone with your lips pursed and your tongue sticking straight out like a torpedo? When I have been on the receiving end of a TT, time goes into slow motion, and in my mind, I have time to let out a bloodcurdling scream. Then it happens, and in an instant, I feel like a fish realizing that that squiggly worm he had planned for dinner had a hook in it, and there is nothing I can do until the unpleasant worm stops wiggling and the unpleasant experience is over. Fire in the hole!

Speaking of fish, the next type of kisser that I have experienced is the Fish Lippers. Picture your goldfish looking at you from inside the tank and his lips are O-shaped and flexing open and closed. This type of kissing is made that much more unpleasant if they are missing teeth or didn't pass on the three-bean spicy burrito at lunch. (Yes, this did actually happen). They move their mouth in that repetitive gasping-for-air motion, and the kiss never strays from its original O shape or open and close chomping movement. Throw this one back for sure.

And then, the be all and end all of bad kissers, are the Flubber Lippers. It feels cold, lifeless, and slimy *all the time*. There were a few men that had no substance behind their kiss. It was like a mushy handshake. I hate mushy handshakes! They give me the willies. I will admit that sometimes while out on a couple of my online dates, I would get to a point when listening to them talk about themselves where I would say to myself, "I really think it's time to kiss this guy because if he can't kiss, I don't even want to listen to him say another word!" Sounds cruel and cold, but I did get like this after a while of doing the dating scene.

One particular date was going about a four on a scale from one to ten, and at one point, I asked if we could kiss. He seemed pleased that I was so "forward" and he agreed. We went for it together, and after the kiss, I wanted to ring the gong from *The Gong Show*. It was like kissing flubber, a mushy gel-like substance that doesn't hold a form and always feels cold, lifeless, and slimy. It was like his lips had no facial muscles. It gave me the willies. I gave him another chance later in the date, but still, *nothing*. I felt nothing. It was like kissing nothing, and I wanted nothing from him. We actually dated a second time, but the kiss was not much better, and that, along with the fact that he was still in love with his ex-wife, made me realize there was not going to be any sort of future for us.

Where was my leading-man kiss?

Chapter 5

My Little Black Book (aka My Purple Love Line Phone)

In an attempt to be safe during my online dating experience, I decided to purchase one of those disposable cell phones with the minutes you can purchase as you go. I asked for a phone number that had an area code in my state that was different than the area code I lived in. I figured I would use this phone strictly for calls from my online dates; that way, they didn't have my home phone or actual cell phone number. So this little device became my little black book, which actually was also known as my purple "love line." Often, it was no more useful than a paper weight or an emergency back-up phone when my smart phone would lose its charge. You couldn't kill this phone. I could throw it across the room (and had on a couple of occasions), and there it would be, in all its purple splendor, mocking me. It was like an annoying miniature Barney singing the "I Love You" song again and again.

In the beginning of the online dating experience, I would only give out this number once I had chatted online through the appropriate site, but after a while, once I did my online sleuthing homework based on any tidbit of information my prospective might have given me in conversation (job, location, last name), I would give him the phone number so we could talk or make arrangements to meet.

I have to admit that it used to excite me when I would hear the single beep tone indicating that I had a text message or the melodic tune that signaled a multimedia message had been received. Of course, I ultimately discovered that most of these multimedia messages included many very graphic (or should I say pornographic) pictures. I had been out of the dating scene for twenty-two years and just had to wonder if this was the latest flirting technique. "Hi, I'm Fred. How are you? Would you like to meet Mr. Johnson? By the way, what are you wearing?"

Even though I dated very few, I gave the number out frequently and had to list the contacts with names that would spark a memory in my head as to who they were. I found it funny that at fifty years old, not only did I have a black book but I had to come up with some system like "playas" of old in order to keep track of who was calling. This new system was instituted primarily because one of my contacts named Ken (Tiger49) had stood me up for a date. I usually would have deleted him immediately, but I suppose I was getting a little cocky and wanted to have a list for posterity's sake. I went on a date with another Ken, (who I liked quite a bit), and we were texting, and I asked if I could call him. He said yes. What I didn't realize is that I had accidentally called the other Ken and told him to call me. So he did and I had no idea who I was talking to . . . *awkward!*

From that point on, I started giving my phone contacts nicknames because all the guys I seemed to be talking to were named Matthew, Mark, Jeff, and Steve. I created names like Bad Hipster, NH Phone Sex Guy, Dunkin Donuts stud, Penpal Dude, Florida Amnesia Man, Sex Fiend, Foot Fetisher, Split Personality Guy, and one I named the Stupidest Scammer on the Planet because he winked at me four times on the same site, on the same day, with four different names, ages, and locations. He had given me his phone number, so I felt I had to call him to offer my opinion about his prowess as an online dating scammer. I politely said, "Man, you really suck at this!"

I discovered that when you have a second phone, it intrigues and scares people. People would ask me suspiciously why I had two phones. They probably worried that I was an unsavory sort, dabbling in the dark underbelly of the world. They would whisper, "Drugs, perhaps? Or maybe a high-paid lady of the evening?" Depending upon my mood, I would make up stories to amuse myself, with my favorite being, "I'm CIA, and I could tell you, but then I'd have to kill you."

Selecting ringtones started out fun. If I liked a particular gentleman, I would assign him a special ringtone so that I knew it was him calling. This song would usually be one of my favorite songs. The problem was that when the guy disappointed me or ended up being a jerk, hearing the song on the radio made me hate the song. I eventually just assigned a default song to the entire phone, so now when one of these suitors called, it played the most appropriate song of all: "Bad Romance." I'm an optimist, but sometimes you just have to be real.

What started out as my love line, full of hope and promise, had started to become a stark reminder that I wanted nothing more than to get rid of this phone, to get off the dating sites, and find someone that I could love and trust enough to give all my real numbers to. I wasn't looking for my next husband, just a friend or companion for now, and if it turned into something deeper, then wonderful. There were none to be had.

Chapter 6

The Firing Squad

I have stepped out on stage and have sung and performed in front of thousands of people. I have taught in front of thousands of students in my lifetime. I have auditioned for parts in numerous shows and have interviewed for many jobs, but nothing, to me, is scarier than a first date. No matter what relaxation techniques I try—deep breathing, exercising, meditation—I can't escape the jitters, which leads to an extreme wave of nausea, which then gives way to abject fear. The knot in the pit of my stomach at the thought of what is to come feels like a lead balloon. My heart is pounding out of my chest even as I write this chapter.

I have often compared the online dating method as catalogue shopping, but when it actually, though rarely, evolves into a first date or a meet and greet, I liken it to a police criminal lineup, or even better, a *firing squad*! (And that's on the side of the one that gets you potentially incarcerated or shot.)

You've texted, messaged, e-mailed, or you've spoken on the phone to your prospective date, and you've decided to meet. Sometimes picking out the right spot to meet is difficult in itself. Most of the dates that I have had have offered to come close to where I live. This is a blessing and a curse. I don't like to meet in my hometown because it's a very small town, and in the time it would take me to order a tea (I don't drink coffee) or a drink or even an ice cream cone, word would have spread, the round robin of calls would have been initiated by some gossipy hen, and the our local free newspaper would be printing it as news.

Going over the bridge to the city wouldn't be any better because I work in that city, my children went to school in that city and participated in scouts and sports, and though I probably wouldn't make the papers—the local city newspaper would find my story uninteresting as they cover more important things like bull chip raffles and the like—there is almost definitely a good chance I am going to see one of my students or a parent or a colleague on one of these dates. So once we have decided on a place, the worst of the CRAP (choices, rehearsal, and preparation) is yet to come.

Choice 1: The Hair

My hair is naturally curly. If I had a nickel for every time someone asked me if I had a perm, I could have retired at thirty and bought my own private island. It is simple to take care of. I wash it, get out of the shower, put a little product in it, and voila, instant curls. I wear it more or less curly based on my mood, amount of morning prep time, or if an outfit warrants a more cute or fun beach casual look.

But when I have the time, I like to straighten it into a couple of nice styles, especially if I'm wearing something more businesslike, theatrical, or cutting edge. The problem is that humidity, rain, or any type of precipitation is the archnemesis to curly hair.

So often, when preparing for a date, I must consult numerous weather stations, radar maps, and various online weather sites to access the hairstyle that I will wear. Then I must determine if I will be in air conditioning or al fresco. Then I must determine if there will be physical activity involved: like, will I have to walk up a flight of stairs or walk down a boardwalk with an amorous date? Normally, these types of activities would not cause a normal person to break a sweat, but as I am experiencing my own personal summer, it is possible to do these simple tasks and look like you've run a marathon. And no matter how well my hair looks when I step away from the mirror, it isn't going to look that way in ten minutes, even with the super-de-duper spray and play hairspray.

Choice 2: The Outfit

I have many clothes. At this point, I have beautiful clothes in many different sizes, but most of my pretty dating clothes are in sizes that I've grown out of and am still trying to grow back into. (Some of you will know what that means.) I try to assess where we are going, the temperature, the atmosphere, and the season, and try to put together the perfect ensemble in my mind. If I had a magazine perfect body, I could put on a paper bag and still look good, but as I am more of curvy, full-figured gal, I must choose and have always been able to pick clothing that flatters my shape.

For example, for one date in the summer, I picked colors like coral and white to compliment my healthy olive-skinned glow and had everything matching or coordinating, including a lovely coral peplum top (which enhanced my boobs, optically whittled my waist, and covered my hips), shoes, and accessories.

I sort my clothes in my closets by color. (Yes, I said closets. I've slowly merged my things into every closet space in my home. It's sad.) I randomly hung my clothes for years. Then I tried to sort them by categories like shirts, skirts, blouses, etc. But I discovered that I actually wake up in a color mood. So sorting them by color has made things easier for me.

Choice 3: Makeup, Perfume, and Accessories

At this point in the process, I have assessed the meeting place, the weather, my hairstyle, and have picked out colors and an outfit I intend to wear. I have showered, put on makeup (not too heavy) in neutral shades and non-frosts to make me look younger (the proverbial "they said so"), and a slight line of white along my waterline to make my eyes appear bigger. I have put on what I call "the miracle," which is primer, which essentially is like spackle to even out your skin, and some bronzer, and a rose shade of color on my cheeks. I use the same perfume that I've used since the eighties because I absolutely love the scent on me, it doesn't give me a headache, and I get compliments on it daily. The only trouble is that when I purchased this scent in the eighties, I could buy it at any department store for $10. Now they don't make it anymore, but there is still a request for it, so you can find partial bottles on eBay for $250 an ounce.

Choice 4, 5, 6, 7, 8, 9, and 10

Unfortunately, once all this is done, the first date is imminent and loads of CRAP (choices, rehearsal, and preparation) start to overlap. In my mind, I start to rehearse my opening lines. I fake wretch into my wastebasket, pocketbook, or any open bowl-like area. And like an over confident actor's ad lib, my raging hot flash makes an unplanned appearance, and I have to run to a fan to keep the sweat from kinking up my now straight hair.

Then I put on the first outfit: the planned outfit, the sure thing. And I look in the mirror, and I hate it! So I take it off and throw it haphazardly on the bed and attempt another outfit, hoping beyond hope that it will make me look fifty pounds lighter than I am. Only I'm not too keen on this one either, so I change and I change, and I put on different bras, and god forbid, I have to wear Spanx because trying to put those on when you are sweating is pert near impossible.

And before you know it, I have a huge pile of outfit rejections, six different bras standing at attention on the bed as if to beckon sailors to use them as sails, and I crumble to the bed in despair in front of the fan so I can cool down enough to find an actual outfit and redo my hair. Changing outfits usually means changing shoes, and now this outfit that I finally have settled on requires me to crawl around the floor of my walk-in closet to find a pair of shoes that matches.

Then the worst part of the process takes place. I start to ponder questions like, "Will he like this outfit? Will he like me? What if he is cruel? What if I sense a very obvious body language snub? What if he says I look nothing like my pictures? What if he stands me up?" And I practice and rehearse my self-defense maneuvers, which usually include snarky comments like, "Well, you're no prize! Meh, athletic and toned my ass," or "No wonder you were wearing a hat in all your pictures!" I would never actually say any of these things, but I feel like I have to put on a suit of armor to go on a first date to protect my heart and my ego. Geez, imagine having a hot flash in a suit of armor. Grr!

Now I am running late. When I was a young mother, and I had to get myself and my three sons ready to go out anywhere, I was always early or on time. Now that I only have to worry about myself, I dillydally and procrastinate on top of the date stress, and I always feel like I'm running late. I get in my car, stuff some money and my ID into the "bank of Rose," and I head off to the date.

The lead balloon-sized knot in the pit of my stomach has moved to my throat now, and I feel like I will blow at any minute. My heart is beating so ferociously that I can feel it in my head, my fingers, and every pulse point in my entire body. And again, I rehearse those nagging questions again and again, except by this point they are much more fearful, and thoughts of driving my car in the opposite direction from my destination offer me a way out. Will he be there? Will he drive in, see me, and drive out? Will he refuse to look at me? Will he be waiting at the outside table like we planned, see me walking toward him, and get up, get into his truck, wait until I can see him, then drive off? Will he be rude or cruel or creepy? I wish I could say that these fears are unfounded, but I can't say that because all these things happened to me. All of them!

I can hear a drum roll from a lone snare drum echoing in my ears, while my heart beats out of my chest in fear. It will be over soon. Then at least I will be put out of my misery. Guns loaded! Ready! Aim! *Fire!*

Chapter 7

It's a Bird, It's a Plane, It's My Diaphragm!

I fully realize that this chapter has probably fallen into the WTMI file (*way* too much information category), but humor me for a few minutes, and then I will try to give you some humor in return. To say I was naïve about certain things after my husband passed away would probably be a gross understatement. I could handle the books and paperwork, I did the day-to-day planning of meals, and taxi services and school applications for college and financial aid, and after some words of advice from my best friend Google, I learned how to do many things I didn't know how to do before.

I learned how to change the headlights in my Miata.I learned the names of all the tools in my toolbox and could wield most of them with great efficiency. But there was no way to prepare myself for being out in the dating world after twenty-one years of marriage. And I had dated my husband for over three years prior to that. So for twenty-five years, I was off the market, and my husband had been the only man I had been with . . . *ever*. (Not for lack of trying on the part of former boyfriends, I might add.)

I was always much more adventurous in the bedroom than my husband was. With him, it was after dark, in the dark, under the covers, and often with him only removing what was absolutely necessary, which usually meant he was still dressed in his shirt (he didn't like the cold) and socks. I drew the line at shoes. I always wanted it more often than he did as well. I am not knocking him by any means. He was very attentive to fulfilling my needs before his own, and he was a wonderful man and husband.

When I found myself alone after twenty-five years in a relationship and marriage, I realized that I knew very little about sex and birth control. After all, I was a nice Italian Catholic woman, and we shouldn't be thinking about such things, right? I had never used any type of birth control. My husband and I were open to having children, and after we had our three beautiful children (with three treacherous pregnancies from hell), we used condoms as our only prevention technique. (Yes, I know, still not approved by the RCC.) We talked about him doing the "snip, snip," but when he decided against it, we continued to use condoms because if I wasn't going to get it as often as I wanted, why should I get a major operation to take care of the issue. At least I wouldn't have to sleep in the wet spot. Okay, I digress.

Another lesson on this journey was that all men aren't created equal. Not only were there different sizes and lengths, but different girths and different pointing directions. What did I know? When an opportunity presented itself with a man I was dating, I told my partner that he needed to use a condom. He grumbled, as *all* men do when they have to put a raincoat on Mr. Johnson, mumbling something about "not having to use one of these since the '80s, it feels weird, it doesn't fit" yada, yada. It was an extremely awkward moment. It didn't fit. His Mr. Johnson was pointing down instead of up, we didn't have gravity in our favor, and during a climactic moment, the condom flew off like a stone from a catapult. It wasn't in the bed. It wasn't on the floor. I shall assume that you can figure out where it was. Luckily, the problem took care of itself, and one Plan B later, I made an appointment with my doctor to discuss some options.

I sat in the exam room feeling like a total idiot. I knew nothing at fifty years old. My doctor put me at ease, and she was very easy to talk to. Because I had had an "oopsie" (my new term), she couldn't start me on anything until we had done a test in a month to make sure I wasn't pregnant. My head was spinning! In the meantime, she suggested a diaphragm.

By definition, a diaphragm is a thin, dome-shaped device, usually of rubber, for wearing over the uterine cervix during sexual intercourse to prevent conception. To me it resembled a bright ivory beanie. It had a flexible rim to make it easier to put in place. Easier, that is, if you are a contortionist and can bend and stretch in every direction without pulling a muscle or getting a charley horse. You can't leave them in place, so before any intimate encounter, it has to be put in place. *The TV and movies lied to me!* You couldn't just be spontaneous; kissing passionately, ripping each other's clothes off on the way to the bed or desk or washing machine. I had to stop, say, "Hold that thought," run into the bathroom, and hope I could get the damn thing in place.

One night, I had anticipated an intimate encounter, and thought I would take care of things before my partner came out of the bathroom. I got into position, readied the machinery, and all of a sudden, the slippery little sucker went flying out of my hands. It's wasn't a beanie at all! It was a bright ivory flying *Frisbee*! It flew halfway across the room! I spouted a myriad of expletives and did the panicked pants around the ankles shimmy to retrieve the thing.

I then had to try to find some water source to clean it. This scene played out three more times, with the Frisbee flying in all directions. Finally, I managed to place it where it was supposed to be. I tried to look sexy as my partner emerged from the bathroom, with the sweat pouring off my face and my heart racing like I had run a marathon. It was then he informed me that the Mexican food we had eaten had given him a case of Montezuma's revenge and could we just snuggle. Snuggle? *Snuggle!* The last thing I needed was to have another 98.6 degree human being holding me close. What I needed was six strapping native men in grass skirts fanning me with palm branches while another spritzed me with cool refreshing water.

Just then, my partner whispered sweet nothings into my ear. "Why are you so sweaty?" Argh. Thankfully, other options were available to me, and I was able to retire the Frisbee for good.

Chapter 8
Gravity's Downfall

Every woman knows that gravity is not her friend. Things that we knew were up when we were younger are now down and out; they sag and droop like never before even when we exercise daily to try to stop the inevitable. I have actually stood at the mirror sometimes for fifteen minutes, bending and adjusting the "girls" so that if it was a tad chilly on a given day, and I had NE (nippleus erectus), it didn't look like one nipple was in Canada and the other was vacationing in Florida. I am well-endowed in the chest department, and when underwire bras failed to lift and separate, I started using a push-up bra with small air-filled balloons that fit in a compartment under the cup to give them a lift.

One particularly amorous date with a man I was seeing ended with an occasion to experience some of the pleasures of life. I attempted to look sexy as I slowly removed my bra and threw it to my right, then made my way in my best vixen walk to the right side of the bed. What I hadn't realized was that the damn balloon had fallen out of the compartment onto the floor. As I was about to slink onto the bed, I stepped straight on the balloon, which popped with the loudest crack I had ever heard. My date thought it was a drive-by shooting and jumped off the side of the bed onto the floor and assumed crash position. Then he exclaimed, "What the hell was that!" And I exclaimed, "Man, that was loud, must have been a car backfiring!" I don't think he bought the explanation. Unfortunately, the "explosion" had ruined the moment for my date, and I saw him periodically peeking out of the venetian blinds to survey the scene on the street. (Maybe he was in the witness protection program.) Things were a little lopsided on the ride home.

I watched gravity's cruel effect daily, but one day, I realized that it truly does affect every aspect of your life. I had gotten a wink from REGGIE06040, and then he sent me an e-mail. Reggie looked really handsome and clean cut and had beautiful blue eyes. He said he had a great job that he loved. (It's always a plus to date someone with a job.) His e-mail was very cordial and sweet, and then he asked me a question, "Do you think it's strange for a person to say that he likes to give foot massages?" Being a person who loves to *get* foot massages, I replied the only way I could with, "No, I love getting foot massages!" Original, right?

Reggie "favorited" me, which is a true badge of honor in the online dating world. We talked on the phone and e-mailed, and when he kept asking about my painted toe nails, and how many pair of shoes I owned, and the fact that his favorite type of shoe for women were flip flops, it was very easy to figure out that Reggie had a huge foot fetish. At one point, he asked me to send him some pictures of my feet, some in shoes and some without. Deep down, I think I knew that I wouldn't really date this guy, so I decided to oblige for research purposes only. They were just feet, for heaven's sake!

I figured that I'd take a few quick pictures and I'd be done. *Not!* I had just painted my toes a pretty fuchsia color and bent over at the waist to take a picture, then another, then another. "It can't be!" I exclaimed out loud. My son asked me if something was wrong, and I yelled, "Gravity!" and his confused response led me to yell "Never mind!" I grabbed my faux fur stole and my dainty gold sparkly sandals and tried to get artistic. I took all the lampshades off my lamps to help with the mood lighting and placed the fur on the ground as a backdrop. My bedroom looked like a storm had hit and left a debris field of lace, furs, and shoes in its wake. No matter how many pictures I took, the result was the same—*gravity* had made my feet look *fat* in every picture! Each picture I flipped through looked more horrendous than the previous one.

My ego was already damaged from some of my online dating experiences, and now my feet were fat, and I didn't have one decent picture to send to Reggie. After all, he had a foot fetish, so he must have been a connoisseur of sorts! Did he like a high arch or long toes? My pictures looked more duck-like than human. I collapsed on my bed in despair. (Okay, I'm being a little melodramatic, but I was a little pissed off!)

Gianna was bored as usual during these rituals I performed often, so during the photo shoot, she decided to paint her own nails, interrupting my little outbursts with inquiries as to where the polish remover was, or which color should she choose, or should she do a French manicure. Gianna had beautiful feet of course. After she decided on her color, 108 Degrees, which was the same color I had on my toes, she nonchalantly suggested that I use my profile picture secret. Why hadn't I thought of that?

In my entire life, I have liked (and I use the term loosely) exactly five pictures of myself: high school yearbook pic, college yearbook pic, engagement photo, one picture taken at a wedding, and my wedding rehearsal dinner photo. Considering that all these pictures were taken in 1988 or before, I didn't figure I could use any of these for my profile though. I have encountered plenty of men who do use old pictures however.

I had found a technique through which I could take a picture of myself which made my eyes look wide and bright, and my chin looked, well, should we say, it just looked like one chin instead of many. I would hold the camera above my head and look up so the light would shine in my eyes and my head would be at a very flattering angle. So I thought why not try it with my feet. So I'm afraid you are going to have to use your imagination and picture me, a fifty-year-old woman, lying down with my feet up in the air, snapping pictures that were sure to garner me a photo spread in "Foot Fetish" or "Man, I Love Feet (MILF for short) Magazine." I changed shoes and photographed away. I tried to add props, but once again, my enemy, gravity, prevented me from throwing objects into the air to stop them in motion thus thwarting my creativity once again.

I finally had some shots to send to Reggie. My favorite was the one in the pink rhinestones, but Reggie preferred the gold rhinestones. He said they made my feet look classy. (I didn't say it, he did!) He said I had pretty feet (I personally think I have the ugliest feet around. They are small and round and my toes look like little sausages. That's why I own so many pairs of shoes), but who am I to argue, he *was* the connoisseur after all!

One day, I went to get a pedicure. I was feeling naughty on this particular day, so I texted him to tell him I was getting the most amazing pedicure. Suddenly my phone lit up like a Christmas tree, with texts asking for pictures and details as to what color I used, etc. The reaction was funny and predictable, and I admit, I knew I would get it. The ladies in the nail salon looked at me very strangely indeed.

I never heard from Reggie again. No promised dinners or foot massages; he had gotten what he wanted, pictures of my feet, to do god knows what with, and I fancy that he doesn't have notches on his bedpost but pictures of little feet. Not cool, Reggie! I am so much more than a pair of *feet*! Humph!

Addendum: After not hearing from Reggie for over a year, I received a text from him the other day. After texting each other for a few days and talking about, you guessed it, feet and foot massages, we decided to meet. I knew I *had* to get a pedicure since I had been neglecting my feet as of late. I suggested we meet in a very pretty local park for a picnic. (It was a gorgeous summer day, so I knew there would be families around.) I actually spent more time on my feet than I ever have in my life. I picked out my prettiest pair of flip flops, white ones with various colored rhinestones on them, made a picnic supper, and headed to the park. Normally, I would have that knot in my stomach, but by picking the place and making the picnic, it took away the "who pays and what do they expect for their money" awkwardness.

I also texted him and said, "Look, it's a meeting. Please show up. No one has ever died from having a twenty-minute conversation with someone." He agreed. And for the first time since I started online dating, I wasn't nauseous. I took control of what I could control and just said to myself, "I am having a picnic with a friend."

He was a nice man. He could hold a conversation, and we talked about our likes, hobbies, and our lives, but I don't know if there was chemistry, and he didn't make me laugh. At one point, he stepped on my toe. I think that was his big "foot maneuver." He apologized and peeked under the picnic table at my feet. He was showing amazing restraint up to that point. I was waiting to see how long it would be before he would sneak a peek at my feet.

I don't think he was impressed. He no longer offered to give me a foot massage. He walked me to my car and went in for the kiss. I must have given an indication. (Let's see, I opened my car door and put the picnic basket inside it. That must be it!) It wasn't bad. He seemed to enjoy it.

The next day, he asked me to meet him for lunch at a vegan restaurant. He is not vegan, but he said he liked to go there every once in a while to get a boost. I perused the menu at home in the hopes that I could find something that I would be able to eat. I had only been to one other vegan restaurant, and I was not impressed. To each his own, I say. But Reggie suggested it, so I wasn't going to complain or reject his idea because that is just not my way, so I gave it a chance.

I drank the tepid cucumber water. I chuckled a bit at the waiters and their skinny beatnik bodies and man buns on their heads. We ordered French onion soup, and I recalled that I had to restrain myself from yelling, "Where's the *cheese*?" And when we ordered our main course, Reggie ordered a wrap, and I ordered one of the specials, which was a basil blossom flower and pumpkin seed pancake with apple butter. Quite honestly, when the waiter explained the specials, all I really heard was a "flour pancake with butter." Note to self: look at the spelling of specials at a vegan restaurant.

The presentation was beautiful (if I was ordering a centerpiece for a wedding), but it had too many plants on it for my taste. There was a large plant that looked like the baby's breath from my high school prom corsage, and I honestly didn't know if I was supposed to eat it or if it was just a garnish. Every time Reggie took a bite of his wrap, long blades of grass would stick out of his teeth and I tried not to laugh.

After lunch, my foot fetisher and I talked further about our hobbies and the theater. And he told me that he very much enjoyed going to the theater. He was excited to tell me about the last show he saw. And you will never guess which show it was: *Kinky Boots*! He didn't really understand why I giggled out loud. It didn't work out, I'm afraid.

Chapter 9

The Dent

One breezy summer day, about five years ago, it was so beautiful that I was able to open the windows instead of feeling that cabin fever of being stuffed inside with the air conditioning blasting. I decided to take a drive to do some errands. My boys were inside finishing their lunch, and I left enjoying that feeling of the breeze on my face.

I opened the car windows and began to back out of my garage to the sounds of a '70s song on my radio. "Beach baby, beach baby, there on the sands from July to the end of September . . ." was now replaced by the crashing of metal on metal, plastic shards, and my own melodic screams of "*Son of a bitch!*" and the laughter and guffaws of my sons watching from the bay window as I backed into my son's white Camry that I didn't notice was parked on the right of the driveway instead of where it was usually parked on the left side of the house.

I caught the edge of his side-view mirror with my back right bumper and passed the point of no return as the mirror made a two-foot dent in my sage green Sienna van with white paint. The sound effects of the crash really made it sound like I had completely flattened my son's car like one of those junk yard car compactors, but in reality, there was only a minute green blemish on my son's mirror and most of the damage was to my car.

"We can't have nice things!" I exclaimed after one of my sons inquired from the window with a sarcastic giggle. "Are. You. Okay?" I left for my errands mad at myself.

You may be wondering why I bothered tell you this seemingly insignificance story, but it came to be significance during my "safari."

In the man book, there is a chapter called Auto Macho 101. It seems that the man code requires that men of all sizes and ages take a modicum of interest in automobiles. My three sons had not received their copy of the the man code when my husband passed, as I needed to show them basics like how to open their hood, how to check the oil, and where to put the windshield washer fluid.

This chapter obviously suggests that the man must have at least a vocabulary of auto repair know-how. I discovered this on my online dating safari. I realized that *every* date noticed the dent immediately. I realized that it was necessary for me to explain the *hows and whos* and the origin of the dent. Then I had to stand there and listen to *every* single date offer to fix it for me while listening to their perfect plan for the best *way* to fix it.

I still have the dent, though many have offered to fix it, but no one has actually done it. I probably can fix it myself by looking at one of those YouTube "fix-a-video using a hair dryer and some dust-off," but now I leave it there just in case I need to see if Mr. Right is actually the one that will finally fix the dent. Perhaps that is how I will truly know if I have met the *right* one.

Chapter 10

Hair Today, Gone Tomorrow

Think of any romantic movie from classic to current, and it brings to mind films like *Casablanca*, *Gone with the Wind*, *Somewhere in Time*, and *Letters to Juliet*. Now imagine your favorite movie couple with their sizzling chemistry and passionate kisses, and tell me if you have ever heard the handsome leading man ask his beautiful leading lady, "Do you have hair, or are you clean shaven?"

The first time I heard this question from one of my prospective dates, I quickly responded, "Well, of course I have hair . . . uh . . . oh . . . *oh*!" I couldn't believe what I was hearing and almost fell off my chair. My inner voice, Gianna, got her panties in a bunch after hearing this question as well and started sputtering and spitting (not literally) and yelling in Italian. She walked out of the room and slammed the door.

Somebody had changed the rules on me while I was married for twenty-one years, and that certainly wasn't fair as far as I was concerned. I would like to think that I keep up with the latest styles by devouring fashion magazines and watching *Project Runway* religiously, but it seems I hadn't learned about the "hairless in the nether regions" fad, or let's call it HNR, until I was forty-nine years old. Not only did I learn that it was popular and the "norm," especially among younger people, but now I discovered that men felt it a normal question to ask you about your coiffing techniques even before you met. Every time someone would ask this question, and I found it was quite often, Gianna would say the same Italian phrase, slam the door, then peek back in and say, "That's awfully presumptuous of him to think he is getting anywhere near that region!" I agreed that the question was extremely inappropriate, except it wasn't just one guy—it was many.

When I was married, I always took care of myself, especially when I went out in public. I *never* went anywhere in sweats and always made sure that my hair was combed nicely and I had makeup on. My nails and toes were always painted; I did my own, so it wasn't like I went for a manicure every week (a much more financially frugal way to go). I had always tried to keep that area very neat, especially in the summer. But when you are married, and especially when you are raising kids, winter becomes the off season, and if you forgot or put off the shave until date night, that seemed to be acceptable.

I am one hundred percent Italian, so hair and its growth has always been a battle of wills, and the hair always seemed to win. I probably have tried every product or device out there to try to win the battle—disgustingly odorous creams, razors, little pieces of plastic with some emery device where you swirl it around the area and it's supposed to leave you smooth. I have a collection of devices, touted on television as the latest thing since sliced bread for hair removal. And then, during the off season, while I was married, I actually tried electrolysis. *That* was interesting! I have a *very* ticklish spot on my right side (only my right), and even though electrolysis is somewhat painful, I was laughing my ass off and I couldn't stop. The hair salon across the hall was probably wondering what the hell was going on in there. Needless to say, the region was so vast and dense that electrolysis was not a viable option.

One day, after talking to my friend, Moonflower (who has three teenage and college daughters), we confirmed that HNR was definitely the norm for today's young daters. My forty-year-old male friend, Jake, who I could talk to about anything, also confirmed that HNR was preferred by *all* men, so I decided to try it.

I purchased the heavy-duty depilatory cream for sensitive areas that was supposed to work immediately in the shower. Nope. So then I got out of the shower, put on the cream, and stood there like a dope with my legs apart for ten minutes so as to not crease any of the cream covered area, and got back into the shower. More came off, but ultimately, I had to try to use a razor to get it really smooth. I had now tried hair removal three different ways, and my NR was not very happy with me to say the least and was now afire and not in a good way.

I looked at myself in the mirror and was extremely turned off. It felt strange. It was definitely a lot cooler, and I could feel sensations a lot more, but I thought I looked like a ten-year-old and I didn't like it.

The next day, everywhere I went, I felt like people knew I was bald down there, and they were staring at me. Of course, it wasn't true, but it felt like it. Then the lovely red "bumpies" showed up, and by the third day, things had started to regrow. It reminded me of when I had the chicken pox as a kid. Each time a hair would pop through, I felt a sharp twinge, and it itched like a son of a bitch. I was miserable. Picture a woman walking through a shopping mall trying to look put together, classy, and sensual, and every couple of steps, she is twitching because she attempted to go HNR. Argh!

Also, to my dismay, there are always exceptions to the norm. Jake was wrong. Not *all* guys prefer HNR. There were just as many who said they liked hair. And of one thing I was *positive*—once it's gone, you can't glue it back on. (A new slogan maybe?)

I had a doll back in the '70s named Beautiful Chrissy. She had hair on her head that you could make long or short by pressing a button on her back. Though I had often wished I could do this with my hair on my head, so I could enjoy shorter styles, but then have it long when I wanted it long, I never thought it was necessary to have that ability with my NR. I was still blown away that this was a topic of conversation started by prospective dates. None of these guys ever actually became dates, so my NR was never up for scrutiny.

"Calgon, take me away!"

Chapter 11

Please Read the Owner's Manual When Wielding Heavy Machinery

Life isn't the way it is on TV. You know, sexy older woman dating a younger man, taking him under her wings and teaching him the ways of the world. In my online dating experience, I have been winked at, poked, hooked, and flirted with by many younger men. I will admit that it is quite an ego booster to get a younger man's attention. You see, TV did wonders for the more mature woman. We are now all cougars searching the bars, the beaches, reality TV, and the online dating jungle for our much younger, tastier, and more energetic prey.

One twenty-seven-year-old wanted to meet me in a Dunkin Donuts parking lot, talk through the car windows, then drive to my house. He said, "Aren't you excited for it?"

"It. Really?" How romantic. I didn't take him up on his tempting offer.

Then during a very dry dating spell, I got a wink from Crass81. His name was Zack. He was a thirty-year-old, who very much fancied older woman. His last relationship had been a three-year, live-in relationship with a forty-year-old woman.

Zack had viewed and winked at me before, but I felt he was too young. Then my inner voice, Gianna, cried out loudly, "Hey, you! Now you can say you dated a thirty-year-old when you were fifty. All the other ladies are doing it or want to do it." So after much dialogue with my inner voice, I agreed to meet Zack for dinner at one of my favorite Italian restaurants.

After having being stood up three other times at that point, I no longer waited for dates inside the restaurant, so I waited patiently in my car. He texted his arrival and said he would be coming out the door of the parking garage momentarily. I was waiting with the ever-so-familiar knot in the pit of my stomach when a boy with jeans, sneakers, glasses, and a Boston Red Sox hat walked toward my car with a big smile on his face. My inner voice suddenly deepened to a W. C. Fields dialect and yelled out, "Get outta here, kid, ya bother me." But, alas, it was my date.

Zack was very nice and very cute but looked very young. He was shorter than he had stated in his profile, adding credence to the online dating adage that whatever height they give you, subtract a few inches. This made him look even younger. The first thing I did after we walked into the restaurant was card him. I wanted to make sure he really was thirty. So here I am in the restaurant, looking at his license but trying to read it without my (I'm too vain to wear them, even though I have about thirty pairs of them) cheaters. I was able to make out the blurry year of birth as 1981, and I thought, *Phew, safe.* Little did I know that my little carding event would be the precursor to many quite embarrassing carding moments at area restaurants and bars we attended as a couple. I purposely avoided some restaurants for fear they would ask me if I needed a booster seat and kiddy menu for my son.

As I said before, Zack was very nice. He was kind of an old soul, and surprisingly, we had many similar interests: music, Broadway shows, movies etc. We enjoyed our dinner, had great conversations, and when we left the restaurant, there was that awkward, "shall we kiss" moment. This is when Gianna, my inner voice, and I had the most dialogue. We opted for the kiss. Who cared that I was in the middle of a Main Street? Gianna yelled, "We are fifty and fabulous, and we don't care who knows it!"

Zack was a sweet kisser, and I felt a bit like a sculptor using my lips to shape his. I bit his lower lip gently at one point, and when he went in for another kiss, I gave him my best, "gently caress his face and pull him closer" kiss. One of my personal favorites, I might add. He left with a big smile on his face and said I was a great kisser. Then the big question: "Can I see you again?"

I do not think people truly realize the awkwardness of this question. You have to sum up an entire evening's events into a split second and decide if you want to subject yourself to this person again—the conversations, trying to remember if he chewed with his mouth open or not, did he pay for dinner? Somehow I formed the word, "Sure," and Zack said he would call me the next day.

My experience on dating sites thus far had proven to me that there was a man code book out there somewhere, and the number one rule of the man code book is you don't talk about the man code book, and rule number two is, no matter how well the date went, *do not* call the next day." So I did not hold my breath. I walked to my car, shaking my head, and asking myself, *What was I thinking?* while Gianna, danced around me, very pleased with herself for talking me into the date, the kiss, and most definitely the agreement to see him again. She gleefully exclaimed, "We're dating a thirty-year-old, we're dating a thirty-year-old!" until I became nauseous and told her to "Stop!"

To my surprise, Zack was the exception to the man code, and he did in fact call me the next day. He asked me to the movies, and we met in the parking lot of the local movie multiplex to see *The Artist*, a 2011 French romantic comedy-drama film in the style of a black-and-white silent film. The film was written and directed by Michel Hazanavicius. I could tell that Zack had gone shopping for some new clothes earlier in the day and was wearing a nice pair of jeans, a new sweater, a very stylish coat, but that same Boston Red Sox hat.

I happen to be a Red Sox fan, but the hat made him look like he was twelve and made me look like his Mo—much older sibling. I resisted the urge to tell him to take off his hat indoors like I used to have to tell my sons at Cub Scout meetings. I asked Zack why he liked older woman. He said, "Older women are much classier, dress nicer, and are sexier than girls my age. They can hold a conversation better than girls my age who are only interested in the club scene and themselves." Okay, I could live with that, and that awkward feeling left me.

Once we were in the theater, we took our seats in the uppermost rows in the corner. The movie had been out for a little while, so it wasn't packed. The movie was entertaining but had subtitles, so you lost something if you were distracted. About three quarters of the way through the movie, I got distracted by Zack's lips and decided to go in for a taste. He seemed pleasantly surprised and wasn't trying to dodge my head like some couch potato husband watching Sunday football.

We made out! Honest to goodness, made out, like in the olden days as my children refer to the time when I was a teenager. I chuckled to myself when he snuck in a boob graze by "inconspicuously" placing his hand where it would be pert near impossible to avoid his hand with my boob. I always said in the assembly line of life, the shoulder, chin, and leg departments all took their breaks at the same time, and the boob department had to make up for it. Needless to say, there is a chunk of *The Artist* that I never saw, and since it was a silent film, my only indication that something important was going on in the movie was the soundtrack crescendo. Maybe I'll rent it on Netflix to see what I missed.

Zack had expressed an interest in Broadway shows. This was truly exciting to me, as the theater is a huge passion of mine. *South Pacific* was playing at the Schubert Theater, so I bought two tickets for the show, and he agreed to buy dinner. One thing I quickly learned about Zack was that he was always cold, and he had a bladder the size of a pea. I could totally relate on the peeing aspect, but I, on the other hand, was fifty and experiencing my own personal summer, so much of our travel time consisted of dueling heat controls. On, off, high, low. When his poor lips would turn blue, I would have to take off a couple of layers, just so he could turn the heat on. On this particular date, we were running late and literally arrived at our seats as the overture was being played. Zack cuddled next to me as if I was his very lifeline to something with a normal body temperature. And I believe the bathroom count for him at this point was already four.

The show was amazing, and Zack was happy to have gotten to see a show that he hadn't seen before. Before we left the parking garage, we started to make out a little. There is still something extremely exciting about the fear of getting caught by someone walking by the car.

Then I found it. The reason why dating a thirty-year-old should have been a wonderful thing. Gianna squealed and began to sing in an operatic voice. I believe it was, "Oh, sweet mystery of life, at last I've found you," in perfect tone. There it was: a very likable shape and size, burning a hole through his jeans, hard, and erect like the Washington Monument. I was like a kid at Christmas. I unwrapped it with a childlike exuberance and stared at my prize. The days of quick car "nookies" were a thing of the past for me, and between bucket seats and a middle console that separated the driver and passenger seats, this wasn't happening now. We were also interrupted by passersby going to the theater for the next show, but I had seen it, and I knew I wanted it at some point in time. Soon!

After the show, we drove around looking for a good restaurant. Periodically, we would stop in a parking lot and make out, and when we finally arrived at a great Mexican restaurant, I went into my best Jennifer Biel in *Flashdance* lobster scene mode. For those of you who have seen it, I am specifically referencing what she was did with her foot. Zack was enjoying the flirting and kept calling me "Trouble."

By some miracle, the planets had aligned on this one Monday, and my son was going to be out of the house (a very rare event), and Zack didn't have to work. (His job required him to work varying shifts, and he never had the same schedule from week to week.) I invited him over. I very much wanted him, and he knew what I had in mind. I dressed in my sexiest outfit and greeted him at the door. Lengthy conversation and a house tour would have ruined the mood, so we got right down to business. One kiss, and Zack was excited, and Zack Jr. was at attention, a divining rod searching for the wetness of my love place. (Okay, that sounded extremely romance novel-ish.) This was amazingly refreshing. I had discovered that men my age, though very interested in sex, had to do a lot more coaxing of their juniors to not be so shy, and they often suffered from what I call "incorrect posture." As a teacher, I fought back the urge more times than not to yell, "Stand up tall and straight, for heaven's sake!"

But Zack was here with Zack Jr. poised and ready. I put on my best seductress and gently tied Zack to my bedposts. I'm a little bit of a drama queen. I blindfolded him and touched and kissed every inch of his body. It was exciting to be pleasing someone, and in my bed, he looked every bit a man and not a child. (I had hidden his baseball hat under the bed so he wasn't tempted to wear it to bed.)

Eventually, I untied him from the bed so I could feel his touch. He was gentle and attentive to my lips and my breasts, and I loved being in his arms, but admittedly, all I could concentrate on was Zack Jr. I wanted him inside me. After all, Junior was attached to a young, spry thirty-year-old. Surely, Zack had read the owner's manual on how to wield such heavy machinery, and he had lived with a woman for three years. Ravel's "Bolero" was playing in my mind (cliché, I know, but one of my favorite songs), and it was in its amazing crescendo part around six minutes, eighteen seconds. All the instruments were playing together, the voices had joined in, and I was anticipating the sounds of the drums and cymbals to bring me to climax. I needed it, I wanted it!

Then suddenly, it was there! Not the amazing climax to our lovemaking, but the annoying fly that flies around your ears while you are trying to sleep, the baby in the audience at the show whose parents refuse to remove him, the loud chewing and sloshing sound that someone makes when they are eating with their mouth open or the ever "pet-peeving" sound of someone popping their gum that reminded you of a mean girl from high school. (I know, get over it already.) Zack didn't know how to use it! He hadn't read the manual or even downloaded the quick and easy cheat sheet! He was fumbling around aimlessly, poking it in a tiny bit, then removing it, then in, then out . . . argh! Is it ever proper decorum for a lady to scream out, "Stick it in already, and stop f—ing around!?" Zack came without much emotion or sound and collapsed to my bed to bask in the afterglow. *My* crescendo, on the other hand, had been interrupted by a cartoon sound effect song: "Wha, wha, wha."

Zack wanted to hold me, and as we were tangled together (which was nice), I finally caught the eye of my inner voice, Gianna, who had been cowering behind the chair in my room. It was her tantrums that had talked me into dating Zack in the first place, and as I lay there totally unfulfilled, I was able to free one hand from Zack's embrace to shoot her a quick bird. She went back to hiding.

Zack and I had a few more dates after that. He wanted me to teach him how to drive a stick shift, which I found extremely ironic and funny. He said his mom tried to teach him but gave up. I had been driving stick since I was sixteen, and I was a good teacher. (And that wasn't a sexual innuendo either.) I tried to use words like, "Don't rush the gears, don't be afraid of it, own it, and stick it into the gear."

People who hadn't driven stick before were usually freaked out by the fact that the car rolled back when you tried to start in first gear on a hill. My Miata caught very well in first gear, but I know it can be scary. Zack had done very well in the straightaways, cornering, starting on flat surfaces, but the hills were a problem. We must have rolled down my driveway backwards at least twelve times while I tried to give him some pointers.

Our last trip out, we pulled to a light that had a bunny hill. Usually, other drivers would pull so close behind you that even an experienced driver would get nervous. But in this case, we had plenty of room. The light turned green, and so did Zack! We started to roll backward. The clutch was sputtering and spitting, and he was panicking. So I did the only thing I could do. I reached over his stick shift, grabbed the emergency brake for a second so the car would stop rolling, and then let it go when he got started.

When we were some place safe, Zack pulled over, got out, and said, "You drive!" The lesson was over for the day. He actually did better than most for a first try.

When we got back to my house, my son had left for work, so I decided we should give sex one more try, as I'm into giving second chances. This time, I wasn't leaving it up to chance or Zack. I have been vertically challenged all my life and had never been able to finish on top, if you know what I mean. My knee to hip ratio, never allowed me to get the leverage I needed to do my part of the job and beer had something to do with the man part.

Zack had a much smaller frame than other men I had been with, plus, Zack Jr.'s army-ready attention stance made me want to give it a try. It was wonderful. For the first time in my life, I could get a rhythm going, and in my mind, I was singing, "I am woman, hear me roar!" while neon signs that read *sex goddess* were flashing over my head.

Just when it was started to get really good, Zack thrust me off of him to the other side of the bed and finished his climax. For a second, images of one of those inflatable tube things, where someone jumps on one side and the person on the edge is propelled into the lake, were repeating in my head. Why? Actually, that's not what I said. I said, "WTF!"

Zack left that day, and evidently waiting for him in his mailbox was his copy of the man code book. We had had sex, I believe, and according to the book, you most certainly don't call the next day. Zack didn't. I thought long and hard (no pun intended) about my relationship with Zack—the awkwardness that never went away, the embarrassing carding moments—and I just knew what I had to do. I tried to reach him by phone, but when he didn't call back, I did something I swore I would never ever do. I sent him a "Dear John" text. And it was over. I never heard from him again.

I thought fondly of him the other day and wondered if I should have been patient and given him a little more training. Then I thought longer and harder . . . and changed my mind.

Chapter 12

Casanova and the Chiropractor

"There is a technique that chiropractors use to adjust their patients' necks. The patient lies on his or her back, and the doctor tells him or her to relax, not likely, and he proceeds to adjust the neck by twisting it until it makes the most hideous cracking sound. The mere thought of this gives me the willies"

Various erotic novels have opened a new world to women as of late. Salacious tales of billionaire Adonises, who lead women into a life of submissive sexual behavior. I myself had read the trilogy in a record thirty-six hours, a process that left me relegated to the privacy of my bedroom because I could not control my heavy breathing and periodic pleasure sounds in the company of my family. These books were a sensation for women everywhere, and men, even if they had not read the actual novels, knew enough about them to test the waters in the sexual deviance department.

In the online dating jungle, I had tried funny, sarcastic, serious, sweet, romantic, and sassy profiles to get me noticed. I tried analogies to football, baseball, fishing, and NASCAR to no avail. I am not saying that I didn't get winks or pokes or flirts, but nothing substantial came from these approaches.

One day, I was in an exceptionally punchy mood and decided to redo my profile. I included all the classic lines about being funny, passionate, caring, etc., but under the interest section, I decided to list spankings about twelfth on the list just to see if men actually read any of the profiles. It seems there are a few that do read profiles, and that particular listed item garnered me some interesting comments and emails.

CASSANOVA1962 contacted me via e-mail and said he was very much interested in me. He was a teacher by profession, as I was as well. This was appealing to me on many fronts in that I have summers off and was looking to have a companion to enjoy things with. We met at a popular seafood restaurant on a Sunday night. Cass was a handsome, fifty-year-old man with black hair, hazel eyes, and a goatee that was black and gray. He lived in the next state, but it was right over the line and was not too far from my home. The weekend before we actually met, I had spoken to him on the phone. His voice sounded young, deep, and sexy. We talked and texted and agreed to meet.

I waited in the parking lot for him to arrive. I still always get that knot in the pit of my stomach right before the guy shows, and my fight or flight tendency is always flight. I want to run away more times than not, but Gianna usually keeps me grounded, somewhat. I saw Cass get out of his car, and I waited until he got beyond my car so that he couldn't do an about face and run back to his car without looking extremely obvious. We exchanged hellos and niceties and proceeded into the restaurant.

There was a small wait, so we decided to sit at the bar until we were called. Because I am short, sitting at high bar stools always makes me feel completely awkward, as if I am a child sitting in a high chair. For me, it is really hard to look cool on a bar stool, and somehow, I always manage to get the only broken barstool in the place, the one that rocks back and forth or inexplicably turns in the opposite direction in the middle of a conversation. Tonight, not only did I have the chair with the turning problem, but I had the only one in the place that didn't have a foot rest to keep myself from turning. So there I am, legs hanging, feeling awkward. Gianna asked me if I wanted to play airplane with my strained peas, and I shot her an "if looks could kill" look. Luckily, we were only there for a brief time before we were called into the restaurant.

Cass was easy to talk to, and we began talking about going back to school after summer vacation. I lamented that school was only a few short weeks away, and he agreed that the summer had gone by too quickly. We started to talk about prepping for our classes, lab experiments (did I mention Cass was a science teacher?), and I asked him how many classes he was teaching. He told me that they changed the curriculum and that it was set up differently. I asked how long he had been teaching and he told me thirty years. Red flag! *Red flag!*

I will admit that math was never my favorite subject, but it doesn't take a math whiz to figure out that if he is fifty and has been teaching for thirty years that the numbers just didn't jive. You can't teach at twenty years old. I questioned the discrepancy, and he said, "I'll have to come clean and tell you that I am really sixty and have been retired from teaching for two years. I accidentally put in 1962 instead of 1952 when I was setting up my profile, and I couldn't change it. Besides, I wanted to date younger women."

Gianna, who had been driving me crazy humming Alice Cooper's "School's Out" during our entire conversation, had now jumped up and was causing quite a stir behind this guy's head. She paced and steamed and entertained me with the children's playground song of "Liar, liar, pants on fire, hang them on the telephone wire." I had to agree with her.

We had been lied to by everyone on this dating journey. And not only did Cass lie, but he perpetuated it by engaging in conversation about teaching that wasn't true. I really didn't think I heard another word he said after that. The voice that I remembered on the phone as sounding so young, now sounded grandfatherly, and his pet name of sweetie seemed old to me now. Sixty is not old by any stretch of the imagination, and Cass looked very young and healthy, but it was the *lie*! The lie changed things.

After dessert, Cass decided to sit next to me in the booth and started to amp up his Casanova techniques. He tried to move his hand up my skirt, though I was wearing my version of the chastity belt better known today as Spanx, and that lycra wasn't going to let anyone in. He moved closer and went in for the kiss. It wasn't bad as kisses go, though Gianna was not happy that I even entertained the notion.

After dinner, Cass walked me to my car and then seemed to change into this new person. Perhaps the moon released his inner beast, but he suddenly got a sense of bravado, and after a few tender kisses, grabbed the back of my hair, turned my head, and went in for a passionate movie kiss. It was quite pleasant. At this point, Gianna had gone into her stealth ninja mode and was trying to fight him off of me with her air karate chops and roundhouse kicks. I didn't sense I was in danger, so I told her to knock it off. So Gianna leaned on my car with her arms crossed and pouted, like a scolded child.

Cass must have started to get the feeling that he was all that and a bag of chips at that moment, so he went in for another kiss. With his body, he pushed me up against the car, grabbed the back of my hair, turned my head sharply, and kissed me. Only this time, I heard it—the sound, the horrific chiropractor adjusting your neck sound; the sound that you only hear in movies when Arnold Schwarzenegger, Steven Segal, or Chuck Norris is breaking the necks of his foes. Gianna, still with her arms crossed, sarcastically spouted, "That's gonna hurt tomorrow. Here, give me your phone, and I'll make an appointment with the chiropractor. Do you think you're twenty? Your bones don't move that quickly you idiot . . . you should have listened to me."

I should have listened to her. The next day, I couldn't move my head to the right. I wrote this chapter in the chiropractor's office along the edges of one of those pain indication sheets where you X your pain spots and give it a one to ten rating. I should have listened to my inner voice. I didn't go out with him again. We tried to get together other times, but it never seemed to pan out. I honestly couldn't get past the lies. Some things have to happen naturally, and my insurance only covers a certain number of sessions with the chiropractor.

Chapter 13

Norman! I've Hit Rock-Bottom

I put off writing this chapter for as long as I could, but unfortunately, the story has to be told. Just like everything in life is a *process* (I've discovered I detest this word), online dating is no different. There are times when you feel hopeful and happy, and there are times where you feel like you are at rock-bottom, and you'll never be happy again, especially after the loss of your spouse.

Even the smartest people in the world have, at some point, done something they regret or something that was so stupid and potentially dangerous that surviving it made them just purely thankful that they got out alive. This was by far the dumbest thing I have ever done in my life, and thankfully, I survived to tell the tale

Dating after divorce is totally different from dating after the death of a spouse. No one judges you harshly if you are getting out there or getting back on the horse after a divorce, but people have very definite ideas and judgments, which they feel free to offer when referring to the latter, my sister, being the most vocal of them all.

I had tried to date around children and their schedules (children are another story), and I had asked my sister if my youngest son, who was sixteen, could stay at her house one Saturday because I had a date, and I wanted to cook for him and entertain at my house. The riot act she read me was one for the books. All about kicking my kids out, and how I shouldn't bring any man into my house. And why didn't I go to his house, etc. That particular date never panned out, but I was so brow beaten by her words that I went into a very severe slump.

I was still on the online dating sites and was contacted by Norman. Psychologically, though, I felt defeated. This is where I also learned that if a person has posted pictures of himself, and he is not smiling in any of them, chances are good that he has no teeth or very few to speak of. And this was the case with Norman.

He e-mailed me, and we exchanged phone numbers and texted and spoke for about a week. Then he asked to meet. Thoughts of my sister scolding me were running through my head, and it was my suggestion to meet him somewhere down where he lived. It was a bright and sunny Sunday afternoon. We met at a Dunkin Donuts, but instead of talking inside the restaurant, we started talking in his truck. Norman didn't seem like a bad guy, but he was missing teeth, and I remember sitting in his truck with the voices in my mind scolding me, feeling like this was the best I was ever going to get. I had a wonderful husband for almost twenty years, and maybe you only get one chance of happiness. Even my inner voice Gianna was silent.

He asked me if I wanted to go to his house (which was just down the street) for a cup of tea. I agreed, though I'm still not sure why I did, and when I pulled into his driveway and saw his old Victorian house, I should have backed out right then and there but didn't. He was a house painter by trade, and there were cans upon cans of paint on his porch, but the entire house was covered in red peeling paint chips. He had a long porch that creaked with damaged floor boards, and the weeping willow trees that flanked the house made it look like something out a horror movie.

And yet I proceeded. He was not at all menacing; he was polite. (All right, I guess even Norman Bates was polite as well!) We walked in, and the inside of the house was far worse than the outside, if that was even possible. Every wall of the house was covered in wallpaper that was faded and falling off the walls, there was water damage everywhere, there were walkers, and potty seats and other healthcare items strewn about. (He had told me that his mother was recently put in a convalescent home.) The home had that "someone was sick in here smell". And every inch of the house had cobwebs that draped down and mimicked the weeping willow trees outside. And still, I walked in and followed him into the living room.

The living room had newspapers strewn about and old faded family pictures donned the walls, and though I kept hearing those judgmental voices playing in my head, I didn't hear my inner voice crying out to me. It was like I was in a totally sober drunken state. I was so needy and defeated at that point, I started to kiss him. He kissed me back like a goldfish opening and closing its mouth for air. Not at all appealing, and the fact that he was missing some teeth didn't help with the disgusting sloshing sound. But before I knew it, I was asking to go upstairs.

Was I that desperate for human contact? The stairs creaked, the cobwebs dangled down and touched me on the way up, and I half expected a scary old woman's voice, yelling "*Norman!*" from the other room. And yet I still proceeded up the stairs. I remember thinking to myself that this is where I would die, and I would never have to feel the pain of my broken heart again. I would never have to worry about providing for my children because they would be provided for by my life insurance, the sale of the house, and my sister, who was designated as their guardian, who obviously could do this job so much better than I could. And even in this desperate state, I still held onto the one bit of humor I could muster and said to myself, "And most importantly, I will *never*, *ever* have to do online dating again!"

Surprisingly, Norman was very tender, and honestly, from what I can remember, I never felt that he himself would hurt me. I wasn't so sure about what else might have been lurking in the house. We kissed and fooled around a little, and though I have suppressed most of the memories of being in that house, I know we didn't make love, thankfully. But there was a moment when it was quiet, and I was just lying there with my back to this stranger, listening to him breathe, staring at the light coming in a window against the discolored and peeling flowered wallpaper that I thought, *All I have to do is shut my eyes, and I can be back lying next to my husband, on a sunny Sunday afternoon, and all will be right with the world.* I felt that if a knife was going to be plunged into my back by a scary man dressed like an old lady, that at least my last memory would be that of my husband, healthy, happy, and snuggling next to me.

I finally snapped out of my stupor and told Norman that I had to get going. He walked me downstairs and asked if I wanted a cup of tea before he left to go visit his mother in the convalescent home. I declined but thanked him. I got in my car and drove home, thanking God that he protected me through a very obvious self-destructive phase. I remember feeling icky and getting home and taking three showers to try to wash off the shame that I felt for putting myself in that position, which could have left my three boys without a mother as well as a father. And I tried not to think about what could have happened. I picked myself up as I always do and moved forward. The best thing about it is, when you hit rock-bottom, there really is no place to go but up!

Chapter 14

By the Number

Boredom has always made me do stupid things. It has caused me to stare at my computer, waiting for my Words with Friends friends to send me another word, while my brain bangs ferociously against my skull, telling me that everyone is at work, so do something else. It has caused me to spontaneously decide to stain glass my front foyer windows instead of tackling the mountains of laundry that needed to be done. It has even caused me to decide to organize my four (yes, four) junk drawers on occasion, always leaving me with a counter of items I should just blindly throw out, but instead I slide them right back into the junk drawer I just cleaned, making it just your run-of-the-mill junk drawer, instead of the intended organized junk drawer.

One fine day, during the summer, in a state of boredom, I decided to sit and I figure out my dating experience by the numbers. Gianna was always bored to tears by these tedious time wasters, so she was napping very comfortably. The feat I had undertaken was probably the worst waste of brain power I have ever expended, and it did the most damage to my bruised ego than anything I have ever done in my life.

Here are the facts:

- 537 days on Snatch.com (not including brief stints on Plentyofjerks.com, BigBonedBeauty.com, SweetMelody.com, Marriedguyspretendingtobesingle.com, and unbeknownst to me, I was a featured beauty on OldGuysLooking4YoungerWomen.com)

- 6345 views (including one woman who thought I'd be perfect for her friend George, and a transgender named Willy who was looking for a woman, who was looking for a man that dressed like a woman but was a wild woman in the bedroom. Huh?)
- 4296 matches for the site I spent the most time on, which sends you an average of eight matches per day. Then you indicate yes, no, or maybe. If you say yes, the match is notified that you are interested.
- 2100 yes responses from me, which may also have included a wink, a poke, a flirt, and in some cases, an e-mail hello. This means 2100 men received notice from the site that I was interested. Come on, it's not like I was desperate and said yes to all of them. I have my pride, you know.
- 4 interests from men that were matched with me on the site.
- 12 pictures of Mr. Johnson_sent to my phone, unsolicited. Some were impressive, but since I didn't have the nerve to ask them to take a picture with him next to today's *New York Times*, I could never really be sure who Mr. Johnson really belonged to.
- 39 profiles blocked because the men ended up being scammers or stalkers.
- 10 guys who only wanted phone sex, which I have discovered I have quite a talent for, just in case it ever became necessary for me to supplement my income.
- 1 guy who only wanted to be pen pals.
- 5 guys who stood me up—never showed or texted that they weren't coming.
- 1374 hours of my time at an average of two hours per day (but most days it was more) used for profile updating, searching, matching, texting, e-mailing, chatting, phoning, dating, picture taking, waiting for dates, preparing for dates, dating.

- Number of actual dates: 10
- Number of guys I felt a connection wtih: 2, but unfortunately they liked me but weren't looking for a relationship. It's a timing thing.

When I finished this little project, to say I was disillusioned and depressed would have been a gross understatement. Meeting people serendipitously seemed to be a thing of the past, and this online thing was the only show in town, so I was told.

With his usual perfect timing, my cousin Rocco called at this moment. He heard the devastation in my voice and asked what was wrong. I gave him the *Reader's Digest* version—one, because he's a man with a very short attention span, and two, because I really didn't want to have to restate the blatant facts that were now staring me in the face on paper. So much time wasted.

In his infinite wisdom, he said, "Don't take it personally." *Don't take it personally?* I wanted to reach through the phone and strangle him. How can you *not* take it personally? On one of these sites, you can see how many people are online at any given time; usually the number is around 450,000. So that means that at any given time, half a million people are online, looking for dates. How is it that comparatively, no one seems to meet someone they can tolerate, let alone meet someone they could fall in love with? I'm not knocking the online dating thing because I do know of couples who have had the happily ever after, but the numbers are staggering. And there seems to be so many people out there looking.

I'm going to stick to stained glass or junk drawers from now on when I am bored. Seeing the numbers dance in front of me, with their little hands making L's across their foreheads, has made me realize I am either hallucinating or I should probably put this chapter to rest and go to bed.

Chapter 15

Sweet Symphonic Sounds

I believe in God. Whether you do is not my business, but in my world, He does exist, He is my creator, and I believe He has an amazing sense of humor. Take alpacas, armadillos, a blob fish, a tarsier, and a sloth. Google them. They are quite funny. They look as if they were created by someone on a Friday afternoon before they were about to take a two-week vacation, and they had just decided to mess with nature. They are beautiful and precious in their own right, but funny just the same.

I believe God has a sense of humor because my sister, Nicky, was the biggest tomboy I knew and had two girly girls, and I am the prissiest girly girl on the planet and I had three boys. So instead of going to dance lessons and buying pretty dresses for daughters, I was relegated to baseball and soccer games and sports dominating *my* TV time. I knew every name of every truck on the road and even knew what a combine harvester was thanks to the Tonka book my son required me to read every night for about two years. You see, humor. (Just so you know, if my boys wanted dance lessons, I would have been okay with that too.) And please don't even let me get started on the lovely visual masterpiece that is a man's hoo-ha because someone was having a good laugh after that one was created.

But I digress. In addition to the rules of dating changing while I was married for almost twenty-two years, I realized that my body was changing the rules on me every day, and I was powerless to stop it. I finally resigned myself to the fact that I had to wear those ugly "cheaters" on the end of my nose simply to read anything with print smaller than the first line of an eye chart; and I'm talking about the enormous E.

I had better wear a tank top or sleeveless dress in the middle of winter, or figure out how to get one of those sexy native men to follow me around with a Hawaiian palm fan in order to keep myself from looking like I had been chased by a bear for twenty miles and he had won. And I have to come up with a better excuse for why when my children get in my car after I have driven it, they get blasted out the side doors from the decibel level of my radio. I always tell them that something must be wrong with my radio because it gets louder after I turn the car off.

But for me, nothing denotes the greatest difference between dating at twenty and dating at fifty more than farting. Okay, I realize that we are getting into the seedy underbelly of dating, but this observation is true and extremely stressful.

What is a fart? According to the dictionary, it is a noun that means a flatus expelled through the anus. And a flatus is intestinal gas produced by bacterial action on waste matter in the intestines and composed primarily of hydrogen sulfide and varying amounts of methane. It is also a verb, which basically means the action of expelling a flatus thru the anus.

Everyone does it; it's a natural and necessary bodily function. While researching this book, I discovered that there are hundreds of websites devoted to farting. There are farting terms, the hows and whys, and numerous sites devoted to the thousands of slang names for the fart, including the *Farting Thesaurus*.

I went to Amazon.com to see what would happen if I searched farting, and immediately 255 book results pooped onto the screen, including *Who Cut the Cheese?: A Cultural History of the Fart* by Jim Dawson, and *The Fart Tootorial: Farting Fundamentals, Master Blaster Techniques, and the Complete Toot Taxonomy* by Dan DiSorbo, a Connecticut author. My favorite title, however, was, *Fartina, the Farting Ballerina*, a children's book by Ainsley Beekersnap.

There were blogs about the six most successful fart techniques for women, the scientific components of a flatus, and historical facts, including the notation that during the Roman Empire, the Emperor Claudius passed a law legalizing farting at banquets because of the health ramifications of holding them in. So if everyone does it, why is it a cardinal sin for a woman to fart?

Since I think devoting one full paragraph to the description and fundamentals of the fart is far more than I ever intended, I think, from this point on, I will use one of my favorite fart euphemisms added to the *Farting Thesaurus* by a chap from England and refer to them as *love puffs*.

Even in the privacy of my own home, if my boys are home, I will go upstairs to my private bathroom because on every occasion that I have used the downstairs bathroom right off the kitchen, even with TVs blasting and their headphones in their ears, one of my sweet boys will yell, "Thar she blows!" every time I sit down to use the toilet. This is followed closely by one of them yelling, "Gross!" or "OMG, Mom!" It's humiliating! Not that my love puffs are loud, but acoustically, my downstairs bathroom would be magnificent for the Mormon Tabernacle Choir or the Boston Pops to perform, except that it is only about a five feet by six feet room.

And quite frankly, I think love puffs are hysterically funny! Even reading all the literature, instruction manuals, and blogs had me in fits of giggles for hours. Not that I constantly partake or indulge in bathroom humor, but it makes me laugh to think that within the genius of God creating the human body, He created a natural function that makes a melodic sound of varying tones, volumes, and nuances that erupts from a person's ass. Did you know that the sound of a love puff has nothing to do with the size of someone's butt cheeks but is strictly created by the size and tone of the sphincter muscle? I know, gross. And if I accidentally break wind, it gets me so silly that it further creates a symphony of sweet sounds rivaling Mahler's Symphony No. 3 in D minor. (Which is the longest symphony ever written, according to my friend, Google.)

And don't get me started on the various positions during intimacy that make it pert near impossible to control any muscles at all.

After you read all the information and become knowledgeable about ways to mask or control the puffing, sadly, you read that no matter what you do, even if you manage to control expulsions during the day, you will puff at night when you sleep and your muscles relax.

Is there no end to the agony of dating after fifty? Now I must stay awake all night so as to not run the risk of expelling a flatus, and I not only have to work out every muscle of my body to try to combat the effects of gravity and aging, but I have to add another exercise to my routine to keep me from putt, putting across the floor or night puffing. Maybe Richard Simmons can come up with a new routine called Puffing to the Oldies, or I can dig out my Suzanne Somers's Buttmaster, or I can try the new Puff 90X. All I know is that dating after fifty is *insanity*.

Chapter 16

The Grand Delusion

I didn't have to be any "smarter than a fifth grader" to realize quickly that online dating was a colossal game show, with booby prizes behind door number one, two, *and* three. I was double dared to attempt this match game, and I fought to keep the hope of finding my love connection without putting my life in jeopardy. To tell the truth, online dating was as chancy as spinning the wheel to find someone willing to take a gambit on an actual face-to-face meeting. And if you were able to arrange a meet and greet, oftentimes it was like, "Let's make a deal," trying to negotiate places to meet and who would pay for dinner. For some of my experience, I felt like I was running the *Amazing Race* as I darted home to check my profile for winks, posted new and exciting profiles, and waited with bated breath to find that perfect match. After all, this had to be better than a blind date?

I didn't ever say I wanted him to be a millionaire. I'd be happy even if he was an average Joe as long as he was a good person, then I'd feel like I hit the jackpot. Simplistically put, online dating is exactly like *The Dating Game* because even though you see a photograph prior to the meeting, the conversations are often awkward, the responses you get from your bachelors can be toe curling, and in the long run, you never really know what you are going to get until they round the corner and are right in front of you dressed in bad '60s clothing. I'm going to stop with the bad game-show speak lest I lose my audience, but you get the picture.

During the summer of my first 537 days, I was invited to my friend, Fiona's cottage that she was renting at Misquamicut Beach in Rhode Island. There was a beautiful view right from the back porch, and the beach is my zen place. It relaxes me and makes me forget my troubles. In addition to Fiona, her husband, Jim, and their daughter, I was introduced to Fiona's friend, Diane, her husband, Kevin, and their three children.

Diane was a psychologist. I have come to the conclusion that I get invited places because, at the very least, I'm funny, corny, and mildly entertaining. So as we enjoyed the beauty of rolling waves, Fiona, Diane, and I began to talk about my dating adventures. Both of these lovely ladies are smart, strong women, who are happily married and have been out of the dating scene for a while, so speaking to them about my dating experiences was an uproariously funny recollection of bad dates, bad lines, and creepy adventures that kept them rolling with the waves.

The next day, I traveled to the beach again, except this time I gathered up profiles and pictures of men on the dating site that I was matched to. My frustration with this adventure has always been that these profiles make these men seem so totally normal, which is often so different from the actual people they are.

So then I got the brilliant idea to make this a game show and let my friends decide which one of these guys I should pick for my next date. I fanned out the profiles and pictures and watched these ladies pour over the information as if they were our only hope of saving the world from a vicious alien attack. They approached their assignment with exuberance and drive, devouring and interpreting each written word. At one point, there were so many papers being tossed about that it reminded me of one of those clear tubes they place contestants in to have them grab for dollar bills as a fan blows them around. The picnic table had become the rejection pile, and the umbrella table had become the place of hope.

I paced back and forth to the final *Jeopardy!* Theme, and after about forty minutes of deliberation, they called a summit to discuss their findings. Alex Trebeck announced the results, and the potential dates were put in order of desirability with only one flat-out rejection. As I approached, I started to laugh. This reaction on my part surprised and baffled my friends, who were sure they had chosen a winner. What they didn't know was that I had added a surprise twist to the *Big Brother* household; I had already been either contacted by or dated all these men or both.

I gave them the litany of creepy experiences I had with each one, and they practically fell off their chairs. In ascending order: runner-up number four was the insurance adjuster who wanted me to send him pictures of my feet (which I did as research, but absolutely no date).

Runner-up number three was a golf pro (I was able to confirm this) whose first e-mail or text to me included a picture of Mr. Johnson taken in his office at the country club he worked for. All subsequent texts begged me to meet him somewhere for sex. (I didn't oblige.)

Runner-up number two was an IT professional for an insurance company who wanted to know if he could watch me pleasure myself from outside my house. (Ah . . . no. What would the neighbors say?)

And the winner was a very handsome man, who touted himself as the quintessential family man, looking for a serious relationship, who asked me to be the submissive in a dominant-submissive relationship, though he was willing to change roles if I liked that better.

Fiona and Diane shook their heads in disbelief. "But they all seemed normal and nice and accomplished," Diane said. I agreed that they "seemed" that way, but this new game called online dating had become a new way for the creepy to get creepier, and there was no way to weed them out just from looking at a profile on a website. Fiona and Diane were not the big winners that day on the Grand Delusion, but, Johnnie, tell them what they've won for consolation prizes!

Chapter 17

The One I Would Have Given My Heart To (aka Starbucks Guy)

Right before I was about to end my online subscription the first time, I was contacted by a man that touted the importance of chemistry in a relationship. He said it was the most important thing. I happened to agree with him, but my experiences to that point had made me feel more leery than anything. His name was Ken, and he suggested that we meet at Starbucks for a cup of coffee, but I had my doubts that anything would come out of it. I didn't know if his definition of chemistry included fireworks, or if he was like me. (I liken it to when Clark Griswold in *National Lampoon's Christmas Vacation* finds the perfect Christmas tree and the chorus swells with a version of the Hallelujah Chorus.)

I waited outside of Starbucks at one of the bistro tables. I saw a black car with tinted windows pull into the parking lot, slow down, and then ride by. My heart sank because I thought he had left, but I didn't realize that there was additional parking in the back. Suddenly, a very tall, dark, and handsome man came up to the table smiling at me. He shook my hand (and believe me, there was chemistry), and he said, "Your pictures don't do you justice!" I smiled, thanked him, and he escorted me into the store.

Admittedly, that was the very first time I had ever set inside a Starbucks. At fifty years old, it was daunting to me. I tried to peruse the overhead menu for words that I understood, but everything looked Greek to me. I figured that I would have him order first and use that as a guide. He ordered a bottle of water (evidently, he didn't drink coffee either), so I wasn't getting any help from him.

I was so nervous based on the fact that this was a first date that on the outside I had started to break into a sweat, while my mouth had gone completely dry. "*Tea!*" Gianna yelled. "You like freakin' tea! Order a tea!" So I attempted to order what I thought would be the easiest thing to order. It wasn't.

I whispered out in a very dry, breathy sound, "I'll have a small—" And the barista interrupted, "You mean a Venti?"

I said, "What?"

He said, "A Venti, you know, a Venti?"

In my mind, I am thinking, "Shit, I got the barista that doesn't speak English, so how the hell am I going to fake my way through this without sounding stupid!" He finally said louder and more "snarkly" (yes, I made that up), "Venti, venti is a small!"

I mustered the courage to finally speak again and said, "I will have a Venti tea!" The barista gave me another annoying look and asked, "What type of tea?" By this point, the sweat was beading down my chest into my bra, and I could feel my hair starting to kink, and I'm thinking, *Hell, if a small isn't a small in here, then I'm sure a regular tea isn't a regular tea!*

And as he started babbling out words like, "Vanilla Chai, Mint Majesty, London Fog, Earl Grey, English Breakfast . . . " I screamed to myself, *What the hell country am I in?* I felt faint. Finally, I heard the barista say something like, "Passion Tango," and I said, "Yes, sure, that's what I'll have!" I figured I had passion, and I loved to tango, so how bad could it be, and I needed this interrogation to stop! When he said, "Did you want regular sugar or sugar syrup? Hot or iced?" I had to resist the urge to leap over the counter to strangle him. I had it hot without sugar. The first sip ripped my tongue to shreds. I guess it really was hot!

We sat at a table in the back of the restaurant. Ken was very easy to talk to. He was funny and had a great smile. We talked about the usual first date things: our favorite things, hobbies, and relationships.

It was comfortable to be with him. At one point, we caught the eye of the woman sitting next to us who had been working on her laptop. She smiled at one of the questions we were discussing. I looked over to her and asked, "How are we doing? Can you tell we are on a first date?" She laughed and said, "You guys are doing great!"

Around 3:00 p.m., after talking for almost three hours, Ken told me he had to drive up to Massachusetts to help a friend who was sick. He walked me to my car. He came closer to me to give me a hug, but he decided to come in for a kiss. It was perfect, my leading-man kiss—passionate and confident, romantic and strong.

He gently held my head and brought my lips to his. And when he sensed my lips had given him permission, our tongues touched with a sensual teasing game. I felt weak in my knees and every place in between. It was by far the best kiss I have ever received. We were surrounding by people going about their busy days, but at that moment, I felt like we were the only two people in the world, and I wanted to get lost in his kiss. When we parted, I was so dizzy that I almost backed into another car in the parking lot. I relived the kiss in my head for the remaining of the day, and I would lapse into a kissing coma just at the thought of it. When he left, he said we could e-mail each other if we wanted to see each other again. Twelve minutes later, I received his email on my phone. It was a *yes*!

The next day, I actually had butterflies in stomach. I dropped him a quick text to inquire about his friend. He thanked me for checking on his friend. Then he sent me a text saying that he was taking a walk, and he said, "Today feels like a good day! It just feels different today!" And he sent back a text with flying hearts and kisses emoticons asking me to call him. He sounded very happy, and I know I was very excited to find someone I liked.

We made plans to meet again that week. But sometimes life throws you a curve ball. (I knew this from experience.) That week, Ken's company had been in the news regarding possible layoffs and reconstructing. There was a good chance that he was going to be sent to Georgia or the Midwest. What had started with so much promise fizzled right out of the gate. I didn't hear from him at all. I finally reached him via e-mail through the dating site. I just wanted to know what had happened. He told me that he was very interested in me, but when his company told him he was being transferred, he didn't want to start something that he couldn't finish.

A few months later, I heard from him. Amid the tumultuousness of his job, they had decided not to transfer him to another state, but things at work were uncertain. During one of our conversations, we talked about some of our fantasies. He explained that he liked to be watched, and he asked me to come over. I agreed. You may think I was crazy, but I knew why I was going over, and I knew what was going to happen when I got there. I wasn't afraid. I was excited to see him again. When I arrived, I let him know I was there. He let me know that I could see him from the window. I peaked in, and there he was, my Adonis, in his naked splendor.

I came into his home and rushed to the bedroom to his arms just like a sizzling hot love scene in a romantic movie. (Okay, I cased the joint first just to make sure I wasn't walking into something frightening. His home was in a nice neighborhood and inside was very nice, neat, manly bachelor in style and décor. There were no horror-movie-style indications that he was a killer, like rope, body bags, weapons, or baskets with lotion in it. I still had my mace in my hand, but my gut told me that I was not in danger. Okay, back to the movie.)

I ran into his arms. He was sitting on the end of the bed waiting for me. He pulled me close to him and started to kiss me. His kisses were frenzied and intense but deliberate and made my body squeal with delight. I felt passion that I had never felt before: Maybe it was the danger, maybe it was me doing something that was completely out of my comfort zone, or maybe it was that I really liked this man and the mutual chemistry was intoxicating. I felt beautiful and sexy in his arms. He was attentive to my lips, every inch of my body. Before I knew it, my clothes were strewn from one end of his room to the other, and we were making love! Honest to goodness, mind-blowing ecstasy, and toe-curling rapture!

When we finished, we fell naked and breathlessly to the bed. We stayed there holding each other. Sometimes we would softly talk, and sometimes there would be no words, only an amazing and powerful connection, and I would get to listen to the sound of his heart pounding while I ran my fingers through the small tuft of hair on his chest. It was as if my body had melted into his and we were one.

At one point, he asked me, "Are you happy?" I didn't have to think about it. *I was*. At that moment in time, in the arms of my leading man, I was the star and leading lady of my very own romantic film, and I was happy. When it was time for me to go, he hugged me long and often, almost as if he didn't believe that I was real. He thanked me again and again for spending the day with him.

We spoke and texted each other after that, but I think sometimes life can get in the way: jobs, families, time. We tried to meet on other occasions, but plans never seemed to pan out. And I believe that online dating can harden a person to the fact that there might actually be someone out there that is right for you, and they might even be standing right in front of you. Ken was the one that I actually felt I could have given my heart to, but I truly believe he was afraid. You can't fake the amount of chemistry we had. But a relationship doesn't work unless two people are willing to take that leap of faith.

Things got weird at the end. He kept asking if he could watch me through my windows or doors. I didn't think my neighbors would appreciate someone skulking behind my house. Fantasies are fine, but I really wanted someone who wanted to be in the same room with me. It doesn't seem to be too much to ask for.

My first subscription ended very soon after this.

Self-Discovery Chapters

Chapter 18

You Can't Get Everything at Walmart

During the tween times after swearing off online dating for good, there was a point where I just gave up looking entirely. I was keeping myself over-the-top busy, performing in theater productions, costuming theater productions, either attending or helping out behind the scenes at theater productions or both, or hiring talent for my job as talent director for a seasonal haunt. I went wherever I was invited. Most often, I was invited out by other couples and felt like the third wheel almost everywhere I went.

One night, on the way back from one of my many jobs, I stopped at Walmart to get fabric for a costume for one of the theater productions I was in. I was wandering the aisles when a man came up to me and said, "Excuse me, I don't usually do this, but I just have to tell you that you are beautiful!" I was surprised and embarrassed and did the "look behind me to see who the hell he was talking to" thing. He asked if we could talk for a while as I shopped.

Now I am an expert shopper, and it is also my therapy after a long or stressful day. I really just enjoy meandering around the store at my own pace or using it as my daily workout. I'm pretty fast with a basket in my hands. I told him I was going to be shopping for fabric, which isn't all that exciting. He still wanted to tag along, which was a little annoying actually. I was not attracted to him at all.

He told me his name was Ron Sands, and he was an engineer for an aerospace firm in Windsor. I felt like he was trying to give me his verbal resume, regaling me with tales of how romantic he was from leaving rose petals on my pillows, to foot rubs, to massages, etc. I remarked to him that he seemed to have worked his way in to my bed pretty quickly for someone whom I'd just met. And there was no way he was seeing that anytime soon.

He asked for my number, and though I didn't feel any chemistry, I at least didn't sense that he was a serial killer, so I gave it to him. I asked him about his most recent relationship, and he said, "Oh, that's been over for months! She was crazy!" Now this statement really irks me to no end. I hate hearing it, and it seems to be the way men describe many of their past relationships even though it takes two to tango. He said he had planned to move in with another girlfriend, but it was too far away from his job, and she wanted him to get rid of his tools because he wasn't a carpenter, and she didn't have room for them, so they broke up. He said his longest relationship was five years, but had never been married.

He continued to walk with me throughout the store, and I really just wanted to shop alone. (I know, I can't believe I was saying that to myself.) So at one point, I actually made the excuse that I had to purchase something in the "unmentionable" department (which was a word my mother used to describe my first bra), and I told him we must part ways, and I ducked down an aisle of bras.

Upon arriving home, I did my due diligence and looked him up on the judicial site and sex offender registry, and he wasn't listed on either. (Always a good sign.) He said he had never been married, which I was also able to confirm through one of the sites. He had said that he owned a house near the Walmart where we met, and his address seemed to check out as far as location, but there was a woman's name listed as a housemate with a different last name, who I assumed might be a sister.

As expected, he called me the next day, and we talked for a while. Actually, he did most of the talking. He told me how attractive I was and what a great partner he would be and again told me of foot massages and drawing me a bubble bath, and once again, I reminded him that it was presumptuous of him to be imagining himself anywhere near my bedroom, and it was making me uncomfortable to hear him talk of such things.

Over the course of this phone conversation, little inconsistencies in his stories started to emerge. At one point, he said he would call me after his class tomorrow. I said, "Oh, what are you taking classes in?"

He said, "Engineering." I reminded him that he had told me that he was already an engineer. And his response was that he was "doing the work" of an engineer so he decided to go to school to get the degree so he could get the pay of an engineer. I asked how long he had been taking classes, and he said this was his first one. Hmm . . . super-de-duper overexaggeration number one. He was only off by about four years or so.

Then I asked about his home and how long he had lived there. Ron said he owned the home with a roommate for about five years, but that the roommate wanted to move to Washington, DC, so they were probably looking to put it on the market soon, and he would be looking for someplace else to live. I didn't question it any further, but the name of the woman listed on the background check was sticking in my head. Finally, he asked if I would meet him for breakfast on Saturday. I figured breakfast is a pretty benign first date.

I met him at a local diner, and when I saw him, I still felt nothing, except now I had that all-too-familiar knot in my stomach telling me this guy was a liar and a yes man. You know the kind that asks you a question like, "Do you like walking on the beach?" And you reply, "Yes," and he says, "I love walking on the beach!" This happened throughout the entire breakfast from him ordering exactly the same thing I ordered to every conversation we had. It was annoying as hell to be with someone who didn't have a mind of his own.

At one point, he reached for my hand. I felt totally uncomfortable but thought pulling away would be rude. So I finally asked him who Ruth was. Well, many things came to light after this question. Ruth was not his sister but a former girlfriend, the one he claimed he had the five year relationship with. He reassured me that the relationship was over. Yes, fella, *that* was what I was worried about. Is this guy for real?

As it turns out, he did not own the house with her, it was *her* house, and he was living in it because he said he would help out with repairs and things around the house. She wanted to sell the house and move to Washington, DC, so basically she was kicking him out of the house and he needed a new place to live. The "crazy" girlfriend must have asked him to move in but couldn't take all his stuff, and it was not a convenient drive to his place of business where he acted like he was an engineer. My place would obviously be about twenty-five minutes closer than crazy girlfriend's house to his workplace.

When we left the diner, he went in for the kiss. I felt nothing. In fact, I think I felt minus nothing. He called that night and asked if he could see me again, and I gave him a lame excuse that I wasn't at all comfortable with him living with an ex-girlfriend because I was quite the jealous person. It was cowardly, I know, but not altogether untruthful. I wouldn't be comfortable if a guy I was dating was living with an ex-girlfriend, and truth be told, I am a bit of a jealous person.

The moral of the story: you really *can't* get everything you need at Walmart. But if you are in the market for a lying sack of doo-doo, who is not really an engineer but "plays one on TV," who is being booted out on his ass by girlfriend number one, but is a beggar being a chooser by not moving in with girlfriend number two because she's too far of a commute from said job as a pretend engineer, then hang out in the fabric section at Walmart. You might get lucky!

Chapter 19

Reading between the Lines: Online Dating at a Glance

The following are a list of terms and observations that you will become an expert at detecting if you wander into the world of online dating.

Profile Analysis: Reading between The Lines

- "I'm a teddy bear"—he's overweight.
- "My favorite thing to do is have a romantic evening at home"—he's a couch potato.
- "To me, it is the thought that counts"—he's cheap.
- "I'm looking for a strong, independent woman"—it's Dutch treat for you tonight, baby.
- "Help me pick out which summer home I should keep in the divorce, the one in Florida or the one on the Cape. I'll e-mail you the pictures of both places"—he's married with kids.
- "I work for the government"—not that there aren't people who do in fact work for the government, but it's probably the number one excuse that men on these sites use to be secretive and lie. "After all, he can tell me, but then he'd have to kill me."

Profile Analysis: Photo Visual Clues

- Hats
  If they are wearing a hat in every picture, they are definitely bald. Not that there is anything wrong with a bald man, but own it already. If you choose to date us, we are going to find out eventually.
- Sunglasses
  Okay, we know you're cool, but I want to see your eyes. Are they kind? Are they mysterious? Are they bloodshot? You can tell a lot about a person from his eyes. They are the window to the soul after all.
- A smile
  A very corny show tune once touted that "you are never fully dressed without a smile." In the online dating world, if they aren't smiling in any picture at all, there is a very good chance that they have terrible teeth, very few teeth, or they don't have any teeth at all. I found this out first hand!
- Instagram filter
  I find it funny that today, with the world of digital advancement as far as photography is concerned, that there is a filter that you can "choose" to turn your beautiful high definition pictures into 1960's faded orangey nostalgia looking pictures. I detest this look, but in the world of online dating, especially dating over the age of forty, this look represents a time when in fact this person may have actually been "athletic and toned" thirty to forty years ago. So *beware*!
- Height
  No matter what they put in their profile for their height, subtract two inches. This is the most difficult to discern because "things may appear larger than actual size!" Photographs can be deceiving, so unless you have a point of reference for the size and perspective of things, like they do in the CSI crime dramas, he may not be as big a man as he thinks he is. What? I'm talking about his height!

- No preferences listed for his date
  Hey, we all have preferences, but I can guarantee that if he has *no* preferences listed on the bulk of his profile that it is *not* because he's so wonderful that he is open to women of all shapes and size—or maybe he is—but he is only looking for sex (he can shut his eyes after all). I had been matched to men mainly because I do in fact have eyes and hair on my head. Their only preference is that his match be five feet to seven feet and ten inches, which means he won't date a "little person" but would in fact date a *giant*.
- No picture
  Plain and simple, this means they are hiding something. In rare instances, you can ask them to send you their picture and they will. And if they send it through the dating site, it may actually be a picture of this prospective date, but there is no guarantee. Most times they are married, or in another relationship, and they don't want their significant others, their friends, or their place of employment to find out what they are up to. In other cases, they only want to converse via e-mail or phone, and this usually, in my experience, leads to phone sex. They have nothing to lose. You haven't seen a picture of them, so they take their chances that they can at least get some satisfaction. What's fair is fair. If you are putting yourself out there, which is difficult to do, they can at least post one picture on their site.
- Too many numbers in their username
  For example, Fred1030045. This is usually a scammer, and they use the numbers to keep track of who they are talking to.

My Psychology 101 Analogies

When you take on any adventure in life, you have to learn from it, or it was just a waste of your time. I learned so much on my dating adventure that I put together a list of terms or definitions based on my experience on the dating sites. I discovered that most of the men that I encountered online fit into one or more of the following categories.

- Peeping Toms
  Men who look at your profile often but don't wink, flirt, chat, e-mail, or ever contact you in any way, shape, or form. At first you say, "Wow, he must really like me!" Then it gets really creepy. Like say hello already, it never killed anybody to say hello. (Unless, of course, you are a real peeping tom, then saying hello while looking in a woman's window will probably get you arrested)
- Pen pals
  Men who enjoy texting or e-mailing, but never want to physically meet you or talk to you on the phone. There could be extenuating circumstances: could be married, could have a girlfriend, or could be still living with his mom. (In a creepy Norman Bates kind of way).
- Diarrhea of Mouth (DOMS for short)
  Men that will talk to or at you for twenty minutes straight about every aspect of their lives, rarely letting you get a word in edgewise. This twenty-minute monologue usually has two outcomes: one, they talk themselves out of meeting with you because that twenty-minute time period has allowed them to *finally* read your profile instead of just looking at the pictures, and they have discovered you are *not* their type; or two, if they have agreed to meet you, and you had to sit in front of them while they explained about their drug addict ex-wife, their schizophrenic teenage son, the girlfriend who moved to Chicago and didn't want a long distance relationship, then *you* want to run away screaming—especially when they thought the date went well and want to see you again.
- Men who have the Eeyore Complex (TEC for short, or men who are wounded and unfixable or WAU for short)
  Both TECs and WAUs are men who have been hurt before in a relationship. (And who hasn't?) But they blame every

new date for the sins of every past failed relationship. They drone on like the monotonous *Winnie the Pooh* character with the pinned on tail. and there is no hope of even attempting to "start fresh" as they will continually lapse back into Eeyore mode. Okay, granted, it's probably got to hurt like hell to have your tail pinned to your backside with a tack, but this little character, unlike most of the men that fit in this category, at least kept trying and plugging along. I had been e-mailing Bo for a few weeks. He was very funny, sarcastic and very playful. He was smart and engaging. My fiftieth birthday was coming up, and I had decided to make it a memorable one. I agreed to do an aerobic exercise routine with my Jazzercise class in front of the crowds at a UCONN basketball game. I had drinks with some great friends, and I had gotten tickets to see a Beatlemania type show at the Oakdale Theater. I decided to ask Bo to go with me and he agreed. I told him it was my birthday. (Quite honestly, it was *not* to get a gift. I hoped that knowing this ahead of time would at least make him think twice if he was going to back out.) He showed. We had a great time! We had a great conversation, really enjoyed the show, and at the end of the night, he remarked about how much fun he had with me. Then we get into the car to leave, and he says to me, "You know, women can't be trusted. Every women that I have dated had lied to me and cheated!" That's when I knew he was a TEC and a WAU. When they had both, there was almost nothing that could be done. He knew nothing about me and already he had unfairly pegged me simply because I was a woman. Some things you can't even fix with a thumb tack.

- Fetish freaks

Men who are only interested in one part of a woman's body to the exclusion of all other parts. Feet guys, ear nibblers, boob men, ass worshippers, nail polish nuzzlers, and I even had one guy ask me to be his mommy. (Ew!) I had even been invited, first message out of the gate, to be in a threesome (me and two guys) while three other guys watched. Um, *no*, I think I'll pass, thank you. He was confused as to why I wouldn't give him my phone number. Everyone has preferences for things that they like on their partner, but I had dated a couple of men who couldn't hold a conversation because they were distracted by my toe nail polish.

- 1-900-FOR-SEXX
  Men who are only interested in phone sex for *free*. I'm sure if you calculated the cost of a subscription to a dating site, and the price per minute for 1-900 phone sex, the true bargain would surely be the dating site because at least they get to look at pictures of "real" women while they . . . (go to masturbationlist.com for the one thousand funny ways to say masturbation—Ben your Franklin and Caress your zesty Zamboni are two of my favorites from the list). But I discovered that being an actress really helped me hone the skills that I didn't even knew I possessed. I did not do it often, but when I was feeling mischievous, I would play along just to mess with them while sitting around in yoga pants, playing Words with Friends, and talking a la Meg Ryan in *When Harry met Sally*. It was quite hilarious at first, but then just it just made me sad that this was all they wanted or needed, and they were content with just talking about sex. What amazed me was the scope of people whose conversations led straight to it. Usually about three questions in: Hi. How are you? *What are you wearing?* (The last one usually was a good indication of where things were going to be headed.)
- Scammers
  Men who make a career out of scamming women (especially widows) out of cash. These bottom feeders prey on the vulnerability of woman. After a while, they become easier to spot. They start with the dears and honeys and the compliments way too quickly. All these men had had their entire family die tragically in a car accident in Zurich. (I may never go to Zurich, it seems a *very* dangerous!) They

usually claim to be self-employed entrepreneurs making $150,000 or more. Their occupations range from porn stars to import or export, but they all claim to be looking for true love. Eventually you would recognize them because often they used the same pictures but change their profiles. In some cases, they have a script of questions that they ask and answer. It is no more genuine an answer than when every beauty pageant contestant answers, "World peace!" to the question, "What do you want in life?" If given enough time, they will ask for money, or for your credit card so that they can come to visit you, etc. If there are *too many numbers in their username*, for example, Fred1030045, this is usually a scammer, and they use the numbers to keep track of who they are talking to. If they ask you to e-mail them outside of the dating site, this is also a good indication that they are a scammer. And if they keep asking you the same questions, that usually means they are a scammer, but they are a very inept one.

Just a Couple of Observations

- Attractive women use these online dating sites to get free meals. A woman commented to me once that she hadn't paid for a meal or had to buy groceries for about six months since she joined online dating. Me, I always bring money because I had been told by one date that depending on how the date went, he decides if the girl is going to have to pay her half of the bill. Evidently, our date went well as far as he was concerned because he paid for the check. I always at least offer.
- After the first experience with online dating, I came up with a new and easy way to weed through the potential dates to give you a great indication of where this date or connection was headed. If the man was willing, I would ask him to play Twenty Questions with me. I told him the rules were simple. At the same time, we each come up with ten

> questions that we wanted to know about the other. Then at the same time, we would e-mail the questions to the other, and we agree to answer them all. I would ask questions like their favorites (movies, food), their families (kids, parents). I always asked about their relationships (longest, shortest, what went wrong), their jobs (what did they do, did they like their job), and their hobbies and dreams (where would they visit if they could visit anywhere?). I genuinely wanted to know these questions, and I wanted to see if any of them had a good sense of humor. (You can usually tell during one of these type of quizzes.)

The most telling part of the game, however, was always in the questions that were sent to me in return. Because we had vowed truthfulness, I would almost exclusively receive questions like: what is your bra size? What is your favorite position? And where is the weirdest place that you had sex? My second stint online was very short, but I can't recall that any of the men I played Twenty Questions with ever asking me about anything but sex. Do men just suffer from a lack of creativity, romance, or an inquisitively nature? Or did they really not care about all of the things that I cared about? And believe me, sex is important, and I like it very much, but that is not the only thing I care about. Thankfully, this game saved me gobs of wasted time.

Chapter 20

Clean-Up on Aisle 3!

I am an expert shopper. I love it! It's magical. I walk around a store, pick up items that I desire, and in my purse is a magic card named Master that makes all my desires come true—my MasterCard that is.

Someone told me that another place to meet prospective dates was at the grocery store. I will admit that in the past, I probably had played damsel in distress if there was a cute guy in my aisle, and I suddenly had an urgent craving for the pickled herring that happened to be on the top shelf. (I've never actually had pickled herring.) I decided to test this theory and set off on my weekly shopping excursion.

After a number of tries, watching men flee as I walked the aisles, I realized that this theory had many flaws. I looked at my basket as I proceeded "manless" to the checkout counter, and I realized that to the observer, it probably looked like I was shopping for seven strapping lumberjacks with the mountain of food in my cart. It really was only about a week's worth of shopping for three teenage boys, but nevertheless, it must have been intimidating to potential dates. So once again, I realized that this approach required finesse, precision, planning, and playful choreography. This was like the *Supermarket Sweep* game show and the rules were as follows:

(Disclaimer: the following rules are simply my observations and not actual rules set forth by any well-known authorities. Therefore, I am not responsible for your experiences, good or bad, or you getting banned from the produce department at Stop & Shop or the Tiggly Wiggly.)

- You *have* to have a put-together look. Classy but not trashy.
- High heels are a must. They make your derriere and hips shake in a flattering way as you saunter around the store, they make a sound so you can be heard as well as seen, and a surprising number of gentlemen will and have commented on my shoes.
- You must move like a graceful kitten stalking its prey.
- Your shopping list must *only* be twelve items or less so you can go to the express checkout line, which is where the single men are. It is rare that you see a man in a line with a full six lumberjack basket unless he is married.
- On *this* shopping trip, you must avoid certain items in the store: toilet paper (certainly it never must be assumed that we take an occasional poop), TV dinner and romance novel aisles (pathetic, lonely-hearts club indication, and most men feel they can't live up to the romantic heroes in those sappy novels), and most especially the feminine products aisle (for obvious reasons!).
- It is perfectly acceptable to linger around the deli. You can make eye contact, chat, and you can do the bend and snap when reaching for the rolls on the bottom shelf and your order on the top. Don't forget the spicy mustard!
- The *meat* section is also a popular area because what guy doesn't like meat, or the thought of a woman preparing him a nice piece of meat. (Insert other meat-related innuendos here.)
- And lastly, it is also acceptable to linger in the produce section, specifically the cucumber section. In my past life, if I needed to purchase cucumbers, I would approach the produce department like a spy waiting for the canister of microfilm with the plans in it for world domination. I would scope out the "cuke" I wanted from a safe distance, search the floor to make sure there weren't any stock boys

> watching, and then I would scoop in in stealth mode and get my cucumbers. Now I had made an art of it. Stand in the S pose modeling position (the most flattering of all stances as it makes you look curvaceous and sexy), place your index finger in your partially open lips and bite on it as if you are thinking, then go for the shape and size that you like. Don't forget to smile with satisfaction before you put it in the plastic bag. And above all, be confident! This maneuver is sure to be underscored with a "bum chicka wow wow" interlude. Well, in my mind it is anyway.

One fine morning, I went into the store on the way to work to purchase something for my lunch, so I was in there at the crack of dawn. (Warning: Do not attempt any of these maneuvers after 10:00 p.m. or before 6:00 a.m. as that is when the weirdoes and vampires come out. Unless of course you are in to that, I'm not judging. Prime date finding time seems to be on a Thursday or Friday night around supper time.) It was about 7:00 a.m., and I walked into the store wearing my leopard shirt, my camel pencil skirt, and heels. (Never underestimate the power of animal print.) For some reason, the store was filled with only men. All the department heads were men on this particular day, and there were many men walking around the store with their twelve-items-or-less baskets.

I walked through the store and felt very much the hunted instead of the hunter. I turned heads around every corner, and at one point, actually heard a man growl at me. One man commented, "Those shoes make you look good!" (Okay, he's not going to win any romantic opening line awards, but I guess I got what he was saying. What I was thinking was, *Great, so if I didn't have the shoes on, I'd be a dog?* I actually started to feel uncomfortable, so I did my shopping in record time but had to take a breather in the feminine hygiene aisle to regroup for my trek to the checkout counter. I knew I'd be safe there. The only woman I encountered in the store that morning was a lovely Indian woman at the checkout counter. I rushed into her line, out of breath, and she greeted me with a smile and a friendly hello. She seemed confused, however, when she told me that the carrots I had purchased were a buy one, get one free, and I refused to go back to the produce section to retrieve my second package. Instead, I ran out of the store with her yelling after me, "But it's *free*!"

Needless to say, I didn't have much luck in the grocery store approach. I see its potential, but who really wants to date someone who was stalking you in the produce department while you were picking out cucumbers anyway?

Chapter 21

Oh, My Goddess!

In the last six months, I have shorted out three—got that, three—of my favorite vibrators. I shorted out the most recent one a couple of days ago. They were aptly named the "Oh, My Goddess" and brought me hours and hours of plug-into-the-wall pleasure. I have two useless battery-operated ones that I never use because the battery life is so short, and I can't stand the helpless moans of the thing as it fights to keep its final battery life. Sadly, they no longer make the "Oh, My Goddess," probably because they shorted out on consumers. (And here I thought it was because of overuse.) I did not hear of a recall, but they probably don't get many people returning their vibrators because of a recall. I suppose the thought of my nether region spontaneously combusting is not a pleasant thought, especially when trying to imagine what I'd tell the 911 dispatch operator in my little town, who is usually a man. "Hello, yes, please send paramedics immediately to my address as my delicate flower is on fire!" And his response, "Lady, this isn't a sex line and is for emergency calls only!"

I was very naïve about anything having to do with sex or sexuality for most of my life. The first PG movie I was ever allowed to see was when I was about fourteen, and it was *Rocky*, and my mother made me tell her why I thought the movie was rated PG. "I guess because he said S-H-I-T?" I replied. Yes, I spelled it out.

While I was still in "my inner voice Shelley" phase of my life—Shelley with her white communion dress and those tapping white shoes—my mother explained sex to me. I was about fourteen, and I will never forget it. My sister and I were helping to load the dishwasher, and she began, "After marriage, when you love someone, the man will stick his penis in your vagina, and he will ejaculate his semen into you, and his sperm will meet up with your ovum or egg, and then it can make a baby."

I remember my reaction vividly. I burst into tears! "He sticks his what, where?" I just thought it was the most disgusting thing I had ever heard. I also had thought that creating a baby was instantaneous and happened the first time you had sex, so I was having none of that. (I have since changed my opinion on this point and have realized that I rather like sex and have a very healthy libido.)

My mother, in her infinite wisdom, also told me that French kissing was a sin! And when the boy I brought to a school dance on my sixteenth birthday jammed his tongue in my mouth, I thought I was going to hell! I was so upset about it that I finally confessed it to my mother, wondering if I'd have to go to confession and confess it to the priest. She said that as long as I didn't do it, I didn't have to go to the priest. Well, it doesn't take a rocket scientist to know that if someone is exploring your mouth with his tongue that things are going to touch, but technically speaking, I did *not* stick my tongue in his mouth, so I was going with that. Finally, I asked my mother why French kissing was a sin. She sat me down on the edge of the tub and said, "Well, French kissing is called 'soul kissing,' and it can lead to (dramatic organ music pause) premarital sex, and that is a sin."

That's when my Sicilian came out, and I started pacing and sputtering, and I could see Shelley waving her hands furiously and mimicking that annoying little "zip your lip" thing she always did, but I was *mad*! "You mean to tell me that I thought I was going to *hell*, that I was a bad person because some jerk jammed his tongue in my mouth, and because it 'could' lead to something else but didn't, etc." I was pissed! But at sixteen, it was probably a pivotal moment in my life because I started to question many things at that point, though I was a little behind the times.

I was still naïve about the sensations I was feeling in my body. I knew that if something brushed across my nipple that it felt really good, and I could see a picture on the cover of a romance novel, and it would give me a twinge. And I started sneaking romance novels into my room and reading them at night when I thought Shelley and my parents might be asleep, and though I never dared breach the unchartered waters of my nether region until much later, I didn't understand the changes in my own body and because I was the Italian Catholic oldest daughter of the church organist, I really didn't have anyone to ask. Because I'm sure it was all a sin, and nobody would ever think I was normal.

Even after I was married at twenty-five years old, I had never ventured to the forbidden forest on my own. One day, probably around the time that I was thirty-two, we purchased a massaging shower head that you could remove from the head on a handle. On one particularly stressful day, while rinsing off in the shower, I had my Madeline Kahn in *Young Frankenstein* moment where I screamed in full operatic voice, "Oh, sweet mystery of life, at last I've found you!" I had my first, wonderful, blissful, stress relieving self-made orgasm. It was mind bending. City water pressure was a godsend! Then I got out of the shower and beat myself up for days. But I slept like a baby that night for some reason.

I felt guilt and shame and thought that my actions were going to bring upon world destruction. I worried that something would happen to my children, and it would be my fault. I thought if my husband found out, he would think I didn't love him, and I would lose him. I resisted doing it again for fear that I would have to go to confession and tell the priest that I masturbated. And then I reasoned with myself, saying, "Well, I never really touched myself, the water from the shower head did the touching."

The shower was my solace place, and though I continued to beat myself up every time I used the shower head, some days I just had to do it. Finally, one day the shower head broke. It was unfixable. And to my dismay, not all shower heads are created equal. I searched, I tried, I bought one, and then another. I made an excuse to my brother, who is my plumber, that there was no water pressure and because my "hair on my head is thick" (it is, but that wasn't why) the pressure wasn't getting the soap out of my hair. He came out and fixed the problem. But though the water pressure increased, the shower head never made me orgasm again. (I changed it six times.)

It was then I discovered a gift my husband had given me one Christmas. It was a little massager kit with multiple heads. One was even heated. I knew it was in the bottom of my drawer, never used, and I thought, well, maybe I could use this, not even realizing that that is exactly what people use these things for. I thought I was inventing something new. I fished it out of the drawer, tried it, and the rest is history.

It took me until age forty to realize that the sensations in my body were normal, and self-soothing was a way to relieve stress. During my husband's nine-year battle with cancer, if I hadn't had my trusty machine, I probably would have killed someone since the stress was sometimes unbearable. I think it has made me a nicer, more even-tempered person. Especially since Shelley was no more, and my new inner voice, Gianna, loves when I take a much needed respite from my daily stresses. I'm not sure who screams the loudest!

What does this chapter have to do with online dating? I've learned that use of these interesting toys can enhance lovemaking for both partners as well. Unfortunately, I learned from my online dating experience that many of these men were just as happy taking care of themselves while thinking about you taking care of yourself, never requiring that you even be in the same room. And this happened so often that I lost count. A phone call was good enough for them. The phone sex that they tried to engage me in was satisfying to them, and they didn't even have to buy me a cup of coffee. (Have I mentioned that I don't like coffee?) You can't learn anything about a person through a phone line. They risk nothing. I like the touch of my man's body, human touch is something I crave. Humans need human touch. Not in a depraved way, in a normal way. I'm normal, for goodness sake! There, I said it!

Oh, hey, I've got to end this chapter now. The mailman is bringing my Amazon.com package to the door with my new Hitachi Magic Wand. Abracadabra! *Spoof.*

Take Two:
Second Time around,
a Glutton for Punishment

Chapter 22

Groundhog Day

I'm not referring to February 2, the day we wait for with bated breath, to see if the groundhog runs and hides after he sees his shadow, which forecasts six more weeks of winter. I will admit that living in the Northeast where the winters are snowy and stormy, I look forward to this day, except when the little rodent tells me I have to deal with six more weeks of winter. But if he doesn't see his shadow, what it does is give me hope. I know full well that even if spring comes early, thanks to his predictions, that there is likely to be one more burst of winter on the horizon which will or has dumped more than four feet of snow on my gigantic hilly driveway. But it still gives me hope.

I am referring to the film *Groundhog Day* that stars Bill Murray. If you haven't seen it, it's a great movie, and it is about a negative newscaster who goes to Pennsylvania to cover the Groundhog Day celebrations. Then he starts living the same day over and over. No matter what he tries—jumping off buildings, running in front of busses—he wakes up every day at six o'clock to the song, "I Got You Babe" by Sonny and Cher. The same thing every single day would drive me insane.

Online dating is like *Groundhog Day*. Let me explain. The first 537 days I was online dating, the first time, I fell into the groove of profile updates, winks, pokes, current pictures, answering quizzes, and e-mails from would-be suitors, it was like having a full time job. When I got off it two years ago, I vowed never to return. I decided to try the "keep myself busy and if it happens, it happens" philosophy. So for almost two years, I went everywhere I was invited, I entertained friends at my home, I was involved in numerous theater productions in all parts of Connecticut, and got an amazing summer-early-fall extra job, where I worked with mostly men. I thought for sure I would meet someone *the fun way.*

By my own definition, the fun way is meeting someone, flirting, teasing (on both parts), thinking about that person and hoping he was thinking about you, finding out he is, exchanging quick texts, working next to that person and feeling the unmistakable attraction, and maybe stealing a moment, whether it be a kiss, or a verbal confirmation of what your heart has already told you.

The fun way is not posting your pictures on the computer like the J. C. Penney catalogue, with different views of your life, a quick write-up of your features (height, eyes, hair, body type), and additional information that hopefully will make the "consumer" want to buy you or take you for a test drive. (Is there a return policy?)

I remember when my youngest son was six. He would wait for J. C. Penney's Christmas catalogue to arrive in the mail. Then he'd devour it with pen in hand. He would check everything he liked then he'd go back again and mark things with an F. I couldn't figure out his system, so I finally asked him what it meant. He said, "I like all the items I checked, but the ones with the F mean fact, and those are the ones I really want to get!" Who am I to question his system? It made it super easy for Santa Claus, I'll tell you that much.

So here I am, two years out; no one special in my life, no dates in almost two years, and I'm lonely. I'm so lonely it's an actual ache! So I decide to test the waters again. Surely, it would be different.

Then I realize that, like the film, I'm existing in Punxsutawney, Pennsylvania, and I'm living the same day over and over again: the profiles, quizzes, winks, pokes, flirts, pics, dates, and best of all, the ego thrashing! I believe they call it being a glutton for punishment. I joined the online dating world again after vowing I would never do it. But there is no place to serendipitously meet someone, and online dating seems to be the only show in town.

In my life, my Broadway extravaganza, I set the stage (put up flattering pics), wrote the script (an interesting but short telling of my tale), picked the title (my username), then opened the floor for the auditions (casting call for the man of my dreams). Then I pressed the send button. Do you want to know the most ironic thing is? The very first match and the very first wink, even though my picture hadn't even uploaded yet, was my pen pal friend I spoke of in earlier chapters—PICME471. He was the first one to contact me my first day on the site. He was the first like and the first e-mail I received.

I communicated with him for a solid year, and he never made a move or asked for a date. I met him once at a football game, he came over, gave me a kiss, went back to his seat, texted that I was cute and then just kept e-mailing me. No date. Nothing. And here it is, two years later. His pics are the same (with a few added), his profile has been changed by a couple of words, but it's the same. The same people, the same pictures, everyone looking for love, and no one seeming to find it. And the coincidence: how in a million years could the first match I received two years later be the exact same one I received the first time I tried online dating for a second time? What had he been doing for the last two years? And he is still just conversing via e-mail with short little questions like, how's the weather? He's loyal as hell, but I'm not paying for online dating to be pen pals with someone.

I thought it was just coincidence in some bizarre universal dimension thing, but then I got matched with Reggie06040, the foot fetish guy, and the one called Tiger49, who stood me up and seems to have remained the same age for the last two years. He never remembered making a date with me, never remembered that he stood me up when he asked me out a second time, and now I'm matched with him again, and he doesn't even remember that any of this even transpired. No, no, and a big fat *no*!

For my take two, I was even more nervous at the prospect of the dates than I was the first time. And my very first date didn't quell my fears. I had met him through a site that was geared to the more mature dater, fifty and older, thinking this would help my prospects.

He didn't like doing all the e-mails and quizzes, so he asked if we could meet for a drink to get to know each other. I picked a nice place near a lake that had a nice outside restaurant. Before the date, I had to go to a friend's daughter's birthday party, and I was so nervous that I couldn't eat a thing, and all my friend's knew I had a date because I was fake retching every couple of sentences or so.

I arrived first and waited for him to arrive. He pulled in and parked, and I waited until he walked by my passenger side before I opened my door. (At the very least, I would have had a good chance of opening my door into his head if he tried to flee.) We greeted each other, and he said, "Let's go inside!" and he began leading the way. Then he started talking to me but wouldn't make eye contact with me.

We walked through the restaurant to the outside patio, and he said, "Let's sit at the bar." I have told you earlier in this book why I don't like to sit at the bar, and this bar was no exception. He popped up into his seat and ordered a beer, while I struggled to get into my "broken" bar stool. He never even looked at me trying to get into my chair. The man sitting next to me actually helped me get up.

Then this Romeo finally asked what I wanted to drink, and I asked for a Chardonnay. For the next twenty minutes, he spoke but never made eye contact with me. He showed me pictures of when he was in the navy, talked about his job, his family. He asked about my family and other pleasant conversation questions, but the entire time we were there, he never looked at me, and it annoyed the hell out of me.

After I finished my second glass of wine, and he finished his second beer, he finally turned his body to face me. Then he suddenly stuck his nose and mouth full into my cleavage, and while holding onto my waist for leverage, he proceeded to motorboat my cleavage complete with full sound effects and head nuzzle, right there at the bar! Then he exclaims, "I really like boobs!"

Who in their right mind would motorboat someone's cleavage on a first date! I screamed to myself. I was dumbfounded and struck mute! Because I was so nervous about the date, I hadn't eating anything at the birthday party, or for most of the day for that matter, and the two glasses of wine hit me like a ton of bricks. My thoughts of pouring my wine over his head and storming out of the restaurant were thwarted by the fact that I couldn't walk, let alone drive, and part of me was waiting for the host and cameraman from one of those hidden "punk me" TV shows to put me out of my misery. No one came. I had to come up with an idea. The only thing I could think of was to pretend I thought it was hysterically funny and make it seem like it didn't faze me. (It did.) He was a *no*. I got home safely.

In take two, I encountered most of the usual suspects as well—the scammers, the creepers, the pen pals, the sex talkers (which if you say it ten times fast will eventually sound like what it really is, stalkers), and then I came to the sad realization that my profile was essentially the same. I was still up there, and maybe guys were saying the same thing about me. My pictures were the same and nothing much had changed as far as my love life in those two years.

Would these repeat customers now think I was more desperate than I was two years ago and feel I was easy prey for their seedy advances? And would I flee again? Yes. I'll probably run away screaming again, or wait until my subscription runs out. Either way, I figured I will feel browbeaten and defeated again. Oh, look, the alarm clock has just clicked to 6:00 a.m., and Sonny and Cher are serenading me with "I Got You Babe!"

Chapter 23

Talked Off the Ledge and an Epic Limerick

When I sat down to write the chapters about the twenty-one dates that I actually had between the two different stints I had on the numerous online dating sites, I wrote the actuals facts of each of date, and not only was it boring but it had such a profoundly negative effect on me that I texted my good friend Deb and told her that she was going to have to "talk me off of the ledge that I was on!" I was standing on this virtual ledge with my manuscript in hand, and I was going to jump and throw away four years of my life down the drain. Every date read the exact the way:

Wink, poke, or flirt. E-mail, text, or call. Hope for a nice guy. Meet and give him the benefit of the doubt. Realize he was a big jerk and a big *no*!

After reading the stories of my dates, I was so depressed, I couldn't handle it. I was mad at myself. I consider myself an intelligent woman, so how could I have not seen this happening? There were men from all walks of life: some were white collars and some were blue. Some were older and some were younger. They were different ethnicities and different sizes, but in the end, it was like dating the same man, and the only thing that ever was changed was his costume.

After Deb talked me down off the edge with my manuscript in hand, I realized, for my own sanity, that I had to find a way to give you the highlights or lowlights of these dates without losing my mind or my sense of humor. The following *epic* limerick was born out of my desperation. I liken this to those videos of an entire epic TV series in eight minutes, only this is in words. The third person narrative is purely to make me not feel as foolish as I did for dating these men. I can try to pretend it really wasn't me. (I know it is called denial.) But each and every scenario below actually happened. So let's start. (You know, get the rhythm going like, "There once was a guy from Nantucket . . .)

Twenty-One

There once was a widow named Rose
Whose loneliness filled her with woes
She joined onto to match
To find a good catch
Now she'll try to regale you with prose

With her profile and pictures in place
She searched for her Mr. Right's face
Twenty-one dates in all
And had hopes for them all
She prayed for, no need for her mace

Wayne, Evan, Zack, Ken, Cass, and Joe
Matthew, Reggie, two Jeffs, Mark, and Bo
Norman, Steve, Carl, Seth, John
Kevin, Chris, Bob, and Don
She'll explain why these men were a *no*!

You have heard of a few in this book
But this poem will give you a look
Of the highlights she'd seen
From say ten or fifteen
Quite truly, she felt like a schnook

Four liked to hear *only* their voice
To be silent was her only choice
Wayne, Matthew, Seth, Steve
She wanted to leave
At the end of the dates she rejoiced!

Jeff gave her a bogus full name
It seemed it was part of his game
He was hiding the truth
Says this amateur sleuth
'Cause he spewed out the lies with no shame

Said he worked for the CI and A
He would not give his ID away
But he gladly sent pics
Of his government dick
"Our taxes at work!" she dismayed.

Evan was born 'cross the pond
Of his accent, Rose surely was fond
So cordial and real
Polite and genteel
And a full head of hair that was blonde

She thought as they supped holding hands
Fin'ly someone that had some romance
Then he asked for a walk
"Just to hold hands and talk"
But had Roman fingers and Russian hands!

Joe thought himself sexy and keen
One Way, Josè, she named him, me mean?
He liked her legs in the air
With some high heels to wear
So he could watch the TV in between

Now the last Romeo was the best
A first date unlike all the rest
Wouldn't look in her eyes
But liked her booby's size
And in the bar "motorboated" her breasts.

Ta-da!

Chapter 24

But Seriously, Folks

I had to devote at least one chapter to *my* commentary on that which is online dating. There may be success stories, but I am not one of them. In fact, I'm sure when I look back on this experience, I will probably chalk it up to one of the worst experiences I've ever had in my life. Maybe it was the age group I fell into at this stage of my life. I think men of a certain age, after getting out of a long-term marriage or relationship, don't want another. They are looking for the quick sex fix or looking for someone to have fun with, no strings attached. They don't really want emotional ties. I think at my age, we are well seasoned in our ways, and maybe we are all a little bit broken by old wounds, hurts, and disappointments in our lives. And though a good portion of these men are *only* looking for sex, they don't hang out on the sites devoted to a quick hookup, an afternoon tryst, or a friends-with-benefits situation. They plague the sites that promise true love and long-term relationships. Why? Be honest at least.

I found, for these men, online dating is like an addiction to porn or to a substance or to anything really. I truly am not judging. The addict can't settle on one page because there are thousands more out there, and they don't want to feel like they missed something. They figure one more hit, or one more snort, will get them what they want and need. Which is what, may I ask? They hide behind fake profiles and fake names. And show up for dates figuring that the prospective partner isn't going to notice that they aren't a six foot three, handsome, athletic and toned, stock broker making 150,000 plus but a five foot six beer bellied, gas station attendant with missing teeth. And that's if you can even get them to agree to a date.

The liars aren't even any good at lying, unless I've become just so good at seeing through their ruse. And people always seem to want what they don't have. I remember, very early in the process, a man who was in his late thirties liked, winked, poked, or did whatever was appropriate for that particular site. He was very handsome and had a very nice body. He seemed very nice and honest, lived in New York City, and owned his own personal training business. We chatted online a couple of times.

He would end up being my first. Not my first love or anything like that. He would be the first guy to want to have phone sex with me. He sent me pictures of his junk, wanted to talk dirty, and even asked me to come to the city. Even though he was surrounded all day by women with perfectly toned little bodies, he was partial to mature women with a little meat on her bones. I asked myself, why would he chance it? Why would he send pictures that included his face, when he owned a business, let alone a business that required personal interactions with his clients?

I had e-mails and chats with him, and at one point, I found his business on Facebook and friended him. He accepted my friend request. Had I been a different person, a mean or vengeful person, I could have ruined him or blackmailed him by posting the pictures and his sexual e-mails. I didn't, of course, and could never hurt someone like that, but the point is that many, many men over the course of my online dating experience did the same thing. They had so much to lose.

I was contacted by a man who said he was an investment banker and very well to do. He said he was getting a divorce. He wanted my opinion on which of his two beach homes he should keep in the divorce, the one on the Cape or the one in Florida. (He even sent pictures of two very nice houses. I'm sure they were lifted from the web.) I told him that it was not my place to give him my opinion on things like that.

He then proceeded to send me full-length nude pictures of himself in a bedroom that included a happy family picture in the background that had a man in the picture that I recognized. It turns out he was the uncle of one of my coworkers. He was married, had kids, had given me a fake name and job, and was not divorcing (at least not *yet*). How stupid. I feel sad for his wife. How long did he think it would take before someone recognized his picture? And again, why would you risk it? I did not tell his secret to my coworker because I didn't feel it was mine to tell, but I prayed that karma did its part.

The scammers prey on the vulnerable. About a week into my first experience with online dating, I experienced my first scammer. His name was Calvin. I can use his name because the chance that Calvin is his real name is nil. The following is his exact profile.

Calvin show us together is a new match

Active within twenty-four hours (forty-nine years old Avon, Connecticut)

- You both go dancing.
- You both enjoy dining out.
- You both like movies.
- You both appreciate music.
- You two enjoy performing arts.
- You appreciate photography.

In His Own Words

> Life is good at this point. I feel I'm a very blessed person. Family values are very important to me. I've been very blessed with loving parents. and i lost them long time ago. I hope someday I'll be able to give the love to someone as they gave to each other and to me. I'm in good health. I enjoy traveling and learning different cultures. I been to many places in this world.

I am shy but outgoing, timid but strong, a loner but loves to be around people. It all depends on who I am with and how familiar or comfortable that I am with them. I am well educated, not necessarily from a collegiate accomplishment level as I am street wise and in tune with my surroundings, making me more often comfortable than anxious.

I would like to find a life partner who believes in living from her heart. A woman who is secure in whom she is and what she feels and therefore does not have to control her significance other or her environment. I am looking for a fellow traveler on this journey we call life. Someone who is not afraid to show her soft underbelly while at the same time can acknowledge her strengths and gifts. I would like her to be dedicated to true communication and expression of feelings, understanding that all relationships take work and nurturance. I would like my partner to recognize that there will be good times and bad times and that life is totally unpredictable. I would like him to be warm and friendly, intelligent, silly and sexy. I would like her to live in gratitude and be dedicated to taking care of her body/mind/soul. I am looking for someone who is passionate about what she believes, knows the importance of de-stressing and can be noisy and quiet. I would like to feel he can help me take care of me and I can help her take care of her and together we can allow the circle to get bigger and broader. I am aware that life is always changing and that it is how we choose to see things that makes the difference of how we move through this world.

His Other Interests

- Books/reading
- Camping
- Cooking
- Fishing/hunting
- Fitness
- Gardening/landscaping
- Hobbies/crafts
- Museums and galleries
- Playing cards/board games
- Playing sports
- Political interests
- Religion/spirituality
- Shopping/antiques
- Travel
- Volunteering
- Watching sports
- Wine tasting

His Appearance

About Calvin and about his ideal match

- Age: 49; 45 to 55
- Ethnic Background: White/Caucasian, Other; no preference
- Height: 5'11"; 3'0" to 7'0"
- Body Type: About average; no preference
- Eye Color: Brown
- Hair Color: Salt and pepper

His Lifestyle

- Smokes: Not at all; no preference
- Drinks: Every once in a while; no preference

- Income: I'd prefer to share this information with my matches later
- Profession/Occupation: Civil engineer

His Background

- Relationship History: Widowed; no answer
- Living Situation: Live with kids
- Has Children: Yes; no answer
- Wants Children: Yes; no answer
- Religious Affiliation: Christian/Catholic; no preference
- About His Religious Background: Details not provided
- Education: Bachelor's degree
- A Book, Movie, Concert, or Play That He's Recently Enjoyed: Details not provided
- Political Outlook: Some other viewpoint

When I started on the dating sites, I had no idea that date scammers even existed. I read his profile as an ODV (an Online Dating Virgin) and didn't question that the information could be completely false. It's only now when I reread it that I question my own smarts. Especially his second paragraph:

"I am shy but outgoing, timid but strong, a loner but loves to be around people. It all depends on who I am with and how familiar or comfortable that I am with them. I am well educated, not necessarily from a collegiate accomplishment level as I am street wise and in tune with my surroundings, making me more often comfortable than anxious."

In other words, I'm black but I'm white. I am tall yet short. I am truthful yet I lie like a rug. How did I not see these words and understand what was happening? I was grieving and vulnerable, and I needed to believe that there were decent people out there. That's why I didn't see it.

We had e-mailed for almost two weeks. He was polite and sweet. As I had said in a previous chapter, he started with the pet names very early in the process. He called me Beauty. At one point, the planets must have aligned and a couple of things happened all on the same day that convinced me that something wasn't right. I had been looking at my account, and there was another man who had notified me that he was interested in me. His picture was totally different, and so was his name, age, and where he lived, but one of the paragraphs in his profile was identical to Calvin's:

"I would like to find a life partner who believes in living from her heart. A woman who is secure in whom she is and what she feels and therefore does not have to control her significance other or her environment. I am looking for a fellow traveler on this journey we call life. Someone who is not afraid to show her soft underbelly while at the same time can acknowledge her strengths and gifts. I would like her to be dedicated to true communication and expression of feelings, understanding that all relationships take work and nurturance. I would like my partner to recognize that there will be good times and bad times and that life is totally unpredictable. I would like him to be warm and friendly, intelligent, silly and sexy. I would like her to live in gratitude and be dedicated to taking care of her body/mind/soul. I am looking for someone who is passionate about what she believes, knows the importance of de-stressing and can be noisy and quiet. I would like to feel he can help me take care of me and I can help her take care of her and together we can allow the circle to get bigger and broader. I am aware that life is always changing. And that it is how we choose to see things, that makes the difference of how we move through this world."

In the meantime, I received an e-mail from Calvin asking what I felt was the most important thing in life. I told him love and family was the most important thing to me. What he didn't remember was that he had me that question on the first day we started to e-mail each other. At that point, I copied and pasted the entire above paragraph into a google search, and it returned pages of hits of date scammers. It was the first time it actually had a name.

A *scammer*! I felt stupid, but I was lucky that I had discovered this early in the game. Others were not so lucky. Others were scammed out of money and their security. Calvin had made a huge mistake as laid out in the Scammer 101 textbook: know your script and keep your patsies straight!

I blocked him and reported him to the dating site, as that is really the only recourse you have as a customer. It doesn't fix the betrayal and self-doubt that it puts in your head however. The scammers just move around, changing things until they get discovered, and they do it again and again. It's a shame really, but it must be lucrative to them because they are everywhere.

I tried every online dating site that was out there, except for the ones known for a quick hookup. After a while, I just started giving the sites my own pet names (this is one of those times you will need to read between the lines): Snatch.com, Plentyofjerks.com, BigBonedBeauty.com, Biology.com, Marriedguyspretendingtobesingle.com, and unbeknownst to me, I was a featured beauty on OldGuysLooking4YoungerWomen.com. Most of these sites have subsidiary companies, so if you belong to one, you belong to all. I was even rejected by a site that was sponsored by a religious group. I believe I answered the question about premarital sex incorrectly. I guess it should have been no instead of "Oh, yeah, baby!"

The worst site for me was SweetMelody.com. After all, they had great commercials on TV, and they seemed to always find that perfect match for everyone. The first time I tried SweetMelody.com, it was a free communication weekend. Free communication was a complete misnomer because communication gave me the illusion that I should be able to talk back and forth for the weekend. This was not the case. I could wink or send questions or write an e-mail, but if any of these Romeos wrote back to me, I would have had to pay for a subscription just to open the e-mail, thus the not-so-free thing.

The love quiz took almost four hours to complete, and there wasn't a time while filling it out that I didn't want to say forget this and walk away! I uploaded pictures and did the usual. And when I got my first set of matches, I couldn't see them until I paid for a subscription.

I found this site to be especially seedy. It was the most expensive and almost seemed like an elite men's club. You couldn't e-mail directly to the member. If I saw someone who I thought was interesting, I'd have to fill out a quiz or a test and send it to the company, who would send it to him, and then he would have to take the same quiz and return it to me. Then they would send you another quiz or test. I couldn't talk to someone via e-mail unless you completed the tests.

I got a few flirts the first weekend (I am convinced they are plants and I'm truly not trying to be a negative Nelly), then nothing, absolutely nothing. Then I kept getting e-mails from the company saying I should change my profile or extend my parameters to include more ages or farther distances. Even without changing a thing, I started getting matches that were hundreds of miles away from me.

I tried to reach the company, but if you try to find a contact phone number, you can't. There are pages upon pages of FAQs, but you can't find a phone number to speak with a real person. In fact, I just tried to get a contact number again, three minutes ago, and I couldn't get one.

I sent a number of e-mails to their contact e-mail with no response, and then finally received a response. I wanted to cancel my subscription early. That's a no-no! They wouldn't do it. They could cancel the subscription at the end of the subscription date. I had to go into my account and hide all my information so that I wouldn't get any more e-mails. (Not from potential dates, because they weren't coming at all, but from the company trying to get me to change my profile or move to Nova Scotia.)

But seriously, folks! I tried them all. I went into the safari the way I face anything that I do, with hope and a lot of humor. I wasn't asking for something that seemed unrealistic. I was looking for a friend, a companion, and someone with whom I had some interests. I was looking for some conversation, some laughs, and maybe some romance. It wasn't on an online dating site.

Chapter 25

The Movie Ending

(Must be read dramatically, background music advised)

Lights! Camera! Action! I have played out the ending of this book so many times in my head, but my all-time-favorite manifestation of my imagination is what I call the movie ending, and it goes something like this.

It's a hot July morning, and I awake from my slumber in my canopy bed that is lined with silk flowers that coordinate delightfully with my border and color scheme (I really have this bed) and yawn gently with a cooing sound so sweet that birds flock to my fingers to give me my first morning greeting. (I don't coo, but a good throat clearing sound usually removes a crap load of morning phlegm.)

I emerge from my boudoir wearing my romantic white gauze nightgown with its wispy off-the-shoulder medieval style flowing sleeves, which is just sheer enough to reveal, to the trained eye, the outline of my sexy voluptuous figure if I move gracefully past a sunlit window. (It's a movie; I'm not going to wear sweats and a t-shirt after all.) And I'm sure it will be no surprise to learn that I do in fact own this dress, and it is in my closet that I have designated for white, and it's far over to the right for some knight, I mean night, when I find Mr. Right. I'll stop rhyming now.

I glide down the stairs and bring a cup of tea to my wonderfully relaxing oasis (my screened in porch), and I sip it gently while swinging on my swing as the gentle but warm breeze makes my face look bright with dew on a spring morning. (Okay, it's more like sweat since I'm probably having my first hot flash of the day, but we'll say I look dewy, and I'd better get back into the air conditioning before my hair kinks.)

Every new day brings hope that I will find the love of my life; that he will be the rose among the thorns of matches in my inbox, a ray of light and hope looking for me as I in turn am looking for him. I float to my office, take in the vision of the birds feeding at the bird feeder outside my bay windows, and turn to my trusted friend, *l'ordinateur*. (It means "the computer" in French, but it sounds so much classier, don't you think?)

I turn it on. I try signing on—nothing. I try restarting, turning the machine on, then off, then on, then off. (Surely if I do it numerous times, it will start working, right? It's the computer equivalent of banging the side of the old console TVs to get the picture to clear up. Um . . . google it!)

As I try everything I know, I feel the rush of panic start at my toes and work its way up through my entire body! (Okay, it could be another hot flash, but let's go with *panic* for now!) "How will I get my weekly message from my pen pal, PICME471? How will I retrieve the myriad of e-mails from would-be suitors commenting on my beautiful eyes, when they are really looking a little lower? What will I ever do with the plethora of free time I will have because I'm not updating profiles, taking flattering pics, answering e-mails, and rating matches?," I rant in despair.

I trudge over to my couch, reach for my landline phone (yes, I still have one), and call the Geek Squad! I am barely audible to the gentleman on the other end, and thankfully, they have the same phone tracking device that 911 emergency uses to track calls because as I explain my dilemma to him, through the sniffles and whimpers, I faint onto my couch into a perfect Sleeping Beauty pose with my hand over my head in despair.

Within minutes (it could have been hours, I fainted after all), there is a strong knock on the door. I faintly whisper, "Enter and save me from this misery." Then I hear another louder knock, and I muster every ounce of energy I have in my body, and I scream in a scream that would make my mother proud (you could hear her call us as children three streets away), "*Come in, the door is open!*"

He enters, but I am too distraught to greet him at the door, and I simply point to my computer room. I hear him place his tools down on the floor, and my heart pounds at the thought that it is unfixable, that I might need to purchase a new one, and wait to see what princes await me.

He speaks to me in a wonderfully sexy deep voice, which for some strange reason reminds me that I forgot to take my Nasonex this morning. There is a slight accent, and I concentrate on the nuances of his voice, trying to get an annoying song from the movie *Shrek* out of my head.

"May I please ask your name?" he calls from the other room. "I like to know who I am speaking to. People these days don't speak to each other, it's a lost art!"

My eyes peak over my overly dramatic hand-across-the-head placement. "I was just saying that exact thing the other day!" I exclaim. "My name is Rose."

"Please don't think this inappropriate, but I think Rose is a beautiful name!" (Sadly, I swear some of my online dates never exhibited the slighted curiosity about me, including asking my name.)

I finally sit up and say, "Thank you!" And he responds with something that catches me totally off guard. "You're welcome." Then he continues to speak in that sexy, Latin voice that is smooth as silk. "Hi, Rose, I'm Tony. My family calls me Antonio, but I Americanized it. How are you today?"

I am finally upright, and I start to foof my hair (you know, that feeble finger attempt to improve the look and style without a mirror or brush), and I say, "I am well, thank you."

And then I sit, waiting for the next question wondering if it will be one of the online dating classics like, "What are you wearing? What's your bra size? What's your favorite position?" And do you know what he said? He said, "How long have you been having trouble with your computer? I should have this fixed up in pretty quickly for you. You know, I fix computers all day, but I'm very rarely on one. Not since I made an attempt at online dating. It was awful.

Liars, cheaters, scammers, and people only looking for a hookup, very shallow people. I even dated a woman for about five dates, and I don't think she knows my last name. They only wanted to talk about themselves and didn't have the slightest curiosity about me."

At this point, I am hearing these words that I have spoken many, many times, and I am hearing the kindness in his voice, along with a sadness or frustration in his tone. And I reply, "I totally understand what you are saying, Tony. But may I call you Antonio? It sounds so much more dramatic."

He replies with a laugh in his voice. "Why, are you a drama queen?"

I confidently say, "Why, yes, I am, but I'm a drama queen that doesn't like drama, the bad kind of drama, anyways."

He responds, "I understand. The job's completed, m'lady," he mused, which made me weak in the knees. I rise up, and our eyes meet and music plays in the background as if on cue. (I believe it is an incoming call on my cell phone but it *was* right on cue!) He takes off his glasses, removes his jumpsuit to reveal his rocking body donned in a tailored black tuxedo, then he removes his tuxedo to reveal an open puffy shirt with tight pants and high black boots, then he takes off that outfit and is standing there in a pair of jeans with a white tank top and barefooted (hey it's *my* movie), and he sweeps me off my feet, looks longingly into my eyes, and says, "Let me take you away from all this!" and he kisses me passionately (a leading-man kiss).

He whisks me out the door in his arms, and I see my three cats tilting their heads in confusion as I am carried away. Through my bay window, I catch a quick glimpse of my computer as I see the webcam focus in on a would-be suitor, who was tapping on the screen, preparing to show me, in vivid HD color, a picture of his junk! Goodbye computer, goodbye online dating, goodbye all you would-be Romeos. I have found my prince!

(Cue music, cue beautiful sunset, cue white horse . . . *cut*!)

Chapter 26

The Tree Frog

My three-month stint back on the dating sites, researching a way to tie together the chapters of my book, had left me once again feeling hopeless, frustrated, and bruised from the ego thrashing. As I still considered myself an optimist, I still couldn't help hoping that this time it would be different. But what is the old adage about insanity? "Insanity is doing the same thing over and over and expecting different results." As the summer drew to a close, I had a way to tie together the chapters of my book, but no one special in my life; no companion, no partner in crime, and no real ending chapter to my book.

I would pass the summer nights meditating on my porch swing and listening to the sounds of nature. One night, I started hearing an odd persistent sound. The first time I heard it, it scared the hell out of me. It was a guttural, burpy-type sound. I enjoy my screened in porch because in my fantasy world, it puts me out in nature but protects me from nature (meaning bugs) being too close to me. And whatever this sound was, it was loud, demanded attention, and sounded like this creature had found a way into my sanctuary.

After research and a visit to YouTube, I discovered that this sound was the mating call of a tree frog. He sang his pining song every night for many hours. And often I would answer him with my song of woe, "I feel your longing and your pain, Romeo." Actually, I named him George. The irony that I was talking to a lovelorn tree frog singing below my tower while writing a book about kissing the frogs was not lost on me.

One hot and humid summer day in August, I was interviewing scare actors for my job as talent director of one of the haunted attractions in New England. The job was exciting, and I loved the people that I worked with.

It was late on a Saturday afternoon, around 4:00 p.m., and interviews were almost over. I was hot and cranky. My naturally curly hair was piled in a mess on top of my head, as I emerged out of my office to fetch the next candidate, and I couldn't wait for the day to be over just so I could get in to the air conditioning in my car.

I had just interviewed a sixteen-year-old boy, and when I stepped out of my office, there was a man sitting in a chair and I assumed that he was the boy's father. But the boy left my trailer and the man remained. As I walked past him to grab a couple of more applications for my office, I suddenly felt an actual breath of fresh air go in to my lungs, and it stopped me in my tracks. (It was ninety-five degrees outside, and I was interviewing in a black painted trailer that was out in the sun all day; fresh air was nowhere to be had.)

He smiled at me, and when he didn't leave the trailer, I inquired to see if he was there to be interviewed for a job for our scare season. I was happy to hear he was there for an interview and invited him in to my office. The connection was instantaneous. He was handsome, and his smile was contagious. His name was Hanz für Frauen. (I know, a mouthful. Loosely, it translates to God's gift to women in German.)

Hanz brought everything he needed for the interview (a big plus in my book since my job was to hire 265 actors, and most did not bring everything they needed to be hired). We began talking and laughing. He told me he was an arborist, a tree guy—as in he climbs trees for a living.

My thoughts immediately went to my lovesick tree frog, George. I remember asking him, Hanz not George, with a giggle if he ever "Tarzaned" out of tree. His answer was, yes, of course. At one point, I got the feeling he was flirting, but since the whole online dating thing had taken all the fun out of flirting, I actually wasn't sure.

I told him that I thought he'd be great up in our redneck section, and I started talking with an exaggerated drawl, and he answered back as if on cue, exactly the way I had wanted him to, right in character. We talked a little longer, laughed some more, he showed me some pictures of himself in zombie makeup, I shook his hand, and he left.

When he shook my hand, I felt a connection, an energy that I have never felt with anyone before. When my boss came in to see me after the interview, he couldn't understand what was wrong with me. I was blushing and couldn't sit still. As if to bring me back to earth, my boss then informed me that I needed to hire twenty actors to dress as zombies for a publicity opportunity at one of the local minor league baseball venues in a week. My first thought was to ask my new tree-flying friend, Hanz, to join us.

In an attempt to maintain my dignity (not that he even knew I was giggling like a school girl), I managed to wait a day before I called him, and I left a message on his machine about the opportunity, and then I posted it on our company Facebook page to get other actors willing to do this promo with me on such short notice. Many of my actors responded with a yes, but the one that gave me the biggest thrill was Hanz's message: "Count me in!" (Okay, not terribly profound, but he did include a little winky emoticon, and I was thrilled.)

To further fuel my inner teenager, he friend requested me. I finally understood why my students would get so thrilled when someone they liked would friend request them. Then I battled with myself. Should I send a message? Will he send a message? Or will we both just sit here like dorks and never even talk?

After throwing a virtual glass of water in my face, I realized that *as* the talent director, I had every right and reason to message him, which I did. It read, "Hi, this is the Zombie Mistress, wondering if you have a costume for Friday, or if you will need some help in finding one." (While dialoguing with some of my actors on the post, they asked if I was dressing in costume, and I told them I was going to be the Zombie Mistress in charge of all of them, and they were at my beckon call.) Zombie Mistress soon became Hanz's pet name for me. He even listed me under it on his phone.

Meeting someone serendipitously was exciting. The flirting, the laughter, the discoveries, and feeling like a teenager again. We also connected on a spiritual level. There was a newness, a primal connection. We laughed at the same jokes and had the same quirky sense of humor. I remember telling him about some of my online experiences, especially about the exorbitant amount of men who sent me unsolicited pictures of their junk.

The day after our first date, I received a multimedia message on my phone. There was a picture, but I couldn't really make out what it was at first. His next message was, "How do you like it?"

I responded, "I can't tell what it is."

He said, "It's a picture of my junk! And that's exactly what it was! It was a picture of an old empty water bottle, some clothes, and a couple of things from the back of his car—his junk! I burst out laughing and knew right then and there that he was going to be different. And he was. I believe we both needed each other at that moment in our lives. We were connected, we laughed, we had fun together trying new things. This is what I'd been waiting for, and I was in a state of bliss, but I was ready for it.

When we started seeing each other, magically the song of the tree frog stopped. It was uncanny. Perhaps he had found his special Ms. Frog. I was reveling in the feeling that I had found someone wonderful. I had fun, affection, and laughter back in my life, and I was elated. However, as the old adage goes, "Love is blind," warned that the red flags were there from day one.

Before we dated, he warned me that the ink on his divorce wasn't even dry, so he was only looking for some fun. But things started to move very quickly on his end, so I didn't question it. His calls and texts were funny and romantic. He was open, and he was comfortable telling me how important I was to him. He complimented my talents, my beauty, and my energy. If we were in the same room, he had to be holding or touching me. The chemistry was intoxicating. We were playful like teenagers.

One night, he walked in my home, and I pulled him in the door, handed him a nerf gun, and told him the zombies were attacking. For an hour and a half, we played and giggled, and I felt young and happy. I loved his playful side.

Some days, we could create these lengthy creative texts like stories or spy novels. Sometimes we would talk seriously about things that had happened in our lives, both good and bad, and it was obvious that he was learning to trust me with things in his life. He was creative and smart, and it was a fun to be with him. He started popping over to surprise me, staying with me a good portion of the week, and asked if he could use my showers if he had a job in the area.

He was so happy with us that he was telling everyone about me. He wanted me to meet his very best friends, and we all had a blast when we were together. He introduced me to his parents, his brother and sister-in-law, and nieces and nephews, and his children (though I knew his daughter before I actually met him), and I adored them all. I was happy to have new people in my life, and my boys saw how happy I was. I was trusting again, which hadn't happened for a long time. We made love every time we were together, and it was wonderful and different than anything that I had experienced before. It was an exchanging of mutual energy, and it was exciting!

As an arborist, Hanz's job was a dangerous one, and I learned from losing my husband that we aren't ever guaranteed tomorrow, so in November, when he was contracted for a job in New York State that was going require him to cut some very tall trees hanging over a steep ravine, I said it. I told him I loved him. I also told him not to overthink it and tried to convince him that I didn't expect for him to say it back to me. It was simply that I believe when you feel something, you should say it, and if those were the last words I ever said to anyone who was important to me, I could live or die with that. I didn't broach the conversation again, but when he came back from his trip, things were markedly different.

I was so full of hope and happy with the new man in my life that I overlooked the red flags that had been there from the beginning. I couldn't see them through my rose-colored glasses. I had learned from my online dating experience that as a person of a certain age, we all come with baggage, and perhaps we are all a little broken.

After I had said the L word, there was a change in him. He became critical, distant, and hurtful. He wanted to control everything that we did or didn't do. If we made plans to meet, and I asked what time he estimated he would arrive so I could get some errands done before, he would tell me that, "If you need to have a time, then we can't get together at all." To me, it was just an estimate and basic respect. Why should I stay home all day waiting for him to come over if I could get some things done prior to his arriving? It was as if *his* time was precious but mine was not. The respect and admiration he had for me was gone. Then he stopped making love to me unless *he* decided he wanted to, and eventually stopped touching me altogether. He wouldn't even hold my hand. He broke up with me two days before Christmas; a Christmas we had planned to spend together with our families. I was devastated by the turn of events.

About six months after he broke it off with me, he stopped by my home on a Saturday, unannounced. (I hate surprises.) He asked if he could speak with me. I let him in. Hanz then proceeded to tell me that he needed to make amends and explain what happened. I sat there and listened to him explain. "We didn't work because I realized that I couldn't control you!" To which I exclaimed, "*Damn, straight!*"

He agreed that he had control issues. I recall him saying that it was possible he was verbally hurtful to me to sabotage the relationship that he didn't feel he was worthy to have. He said he had fun with me. He also said he hadn't had sex with anyone since we broke up, and he had no desire to have sex. Why would he add that to the conversation? Was that supposed to make me feel better? Had sex with me been so bad that I had ruined this poor man? Was there an apology or amend in there somewhere and I just missed it? The conversation may have helped him move on, but quite frankly, it just added another splinter to my already broken heart.

He had some issues as we all do. He wasn't ready for a relationship, and I truly understood. I forgave him because I knew I had to in order for me to heal and move on, and most especially, I had to accept that he wasn't a tree frog that was going to turn into a prince.

Chapter 27

My Stroke of Luck

After my tree frog hopped away, I immersed myself in work again. I was experiencing an exorbitant amount of stress at my two main jobs, as a teacher and a talent director, but that didn't stop me from taking on more jobs for myself. After all, in my mind, if I kept myself busy, I wouldn't have to feel the pain of yet another broken heart. Denial will do that to you.

But stress is a monster, and this monster was stalking his prey in earnest. I was ignoring the effects that stress was having on my body and mind. I couldn't catch my breath. It felt like this monster was sitting on my chest. I also couldn't walk any distance without completely feeling winded. Then one fall day, I called in sick to school because I felt terrible. I had no intention of going to the doctor's however. I was simply going to stay home and rest.

But a little divine intervention, and my inner voice, Gianna, kept nagging me to go to the doctor's office. I arrived at the doctor's at 2:45 p.m., and at 2:50 p.m., I started having a stroke due to atrial fibrillation, right there in the office. I couldn't answer any of the doctor's questions. The words wouldn't come out. I was giving out phone numbers, but none of the numbers were in the right order. The stroke had affected my speech and some of my memory, but thankfully, there was no paralysis or other side effects from the stroke.

The day was a whirlwind of doctors and nurses, tests and machines, poking and prodding, and most of it made me feel like I was again in the depths of that jungle tangled in a maze of vines. But Gianna was there with me, and all I can remember is hearing her say, "You got this, baby!" That night, when I was finally in my hospital room, Gianna and I started talking about memories.

I started with my family: husband, my sons, my parents and siblings, their names, birthdays, anniversaries, even deaths. I thought especially of my late husband and our wedding, the birth of our children, and the fact that he always made me giggle like a schoolgirl. I even thought of the long battle he waged over the cancer, and remembered that we had so many more joys than sorrows in our twenty-one years as a married couple and parents to my three wonderful boys.

I remembered my prayers (the nuns would be happy about that), and I remembered how to draw my sacred Reiki symbols. I stumbled over the pledge of allegiance. I could start it perfectly, but I couldn't remember the last few lines. It was frustrating, but I figured it would come back eventually.

I started naming my friends and funny things about them that I remembered. I started listing in my mind all of my favorites, like pizza and cannoli and *The Princess Bride*.

Then we talked about how scary the day had been, and I thought about what would have happened if I didn't go to the doctor's when I did. I would have had my stroke at home in my bed. My three cats are great company, but as far as I know, not one of them knows CPR or knows how to dial 911. No one would have found me for days. I could have died, or worse, I could have been left in a vegetative state or been eaten by my cats. Imagine the headline: "Woman is Fancy Feast for her Friskie Felines" or maybe "No 9 Lives for Women Eaten As Cat Chow." Gianna was happy to see that I hadn't lost my sense of humor. I finally drifted to sleep at 3:00 a.m. with Gianna protectively watching over me, and I was thankful to be alive.

The ten months after the stroke were probably the most difficult of my life. I remember posting a meme on social media that summed it up perfectly. It read, "Not all scars show. Not all wounds heal. Not all illnesses can be seen. Not all pain is obvious. Remember this before you judge someone."

Because there was no outward paralysis, to the world it looked like I was perfectly fine. But I wasn't fine. I was in constant physical and emotional pain. I was on six new medications, all with their own set of side effects, which included little ditties like body aches, tiredness, and making everything I attempted to eat taste like eating milk-fed cardboard with a delicate Bearnaise sauce made of plastic, rust, and aluminum foil. Every joint in my body hurt, and I walked around my house as if I had just gotten hit by a Mack truck.

It physically hurt my head to work so hard to get words out, and when I got so frustrated from working so hard, I would start to cry. (Thankfully the nurse explained that the uncontrollable crying was probably also caused from the stroke.) I worked on pages upon pages of worksheets for my speech as well as working on my computer. I had to color and read aloud and did whatever I could to do to improve my speech.

Gianna, at this point, had now taken on the role of my personal trainer, and she donned some very loud and colorful Jane Fonda eighties-style workout gear, including headbands, high-top aerobic shoes, and leg warmers to stay in character. She was relentless!

Over the course of my rehabilitation, I realized that something was happening to me that I could have never imagined would happen. I had put away all ideas of dating on the back burner because I had to concentrate on healing myself. I meditated two or three times a day and used my Reiki to help me deal with the pain. The stress monster wasn't stalking me anymore. I continued to work on my own speech therapy and started singing again. (Though the catalogue of memorized lyrics that I previously held was somewhat diminished, the tunes and melodies were there, and for that I was thankful.) But all my therapy was done in the privacy of my home.

In January, my friend, Susan, did something for me that changed my life. I don't really think that she realized just how much it meant to me and how much it helped me to heal. Susan was directing a show at a local community theater, and she asked me to be her costume designer for the production. I had been sewing and costuming shows from the time I was a child, and it was truly a passion of mine.

But since the stroke, I admitted that I was hiding myself in the safety of my home so that I wouldn't have to speak in front of other people.

Her confidence in me helped me to not hide anymore. I was frightened, but I didn't hesitate when she asked me to help. It was an amazing experience, and though I had a couple of frightening moments—the first dress rehearsal, I had to sit with Susan and the rest of the cast to review the costumes, and I couldn't think of the word for *shirt*—Susan, who knew what I had been through, helped me get through the moment, and the rest of the run was wonderful. I met some amazing new friends who appreciated me and my talents. I was able to create and construct costumes and accessories, which I loved, and I continue to work with them today.

For Valentine's Day, for the first time in my life, I was celebrating *love*. I got up, dressed in my fluffy robe, made myself some bacon (it was a special day) and a couple of pancakes shaped in a heart, and placed a single red rose by my plate. I poured myself a glass of mimosa, and I toasted to myself. "Rose, I love you, welcome to life!"

I finally loved *me*. I was lucky to have a second chance at life. I had worked so hard to help myself heal. I had taken classes in Reiki to improve my life, and I had a wonderful family and wonderful friends that loved me. I had talents and opportunities to change my path if I wanted to, and the future was an exciting prospect for me. I finally had the strength to finish my book. I don't recommend going the stroke route to get a point across or to have that aha moment. Though it is cliché, I realized that you really have to take care of yourself and love yourself before you can love anyone else.

I had a follow-up with my cardiologist yesterday, and my cardiologist said my heart was at one hundred percent! He left the exam room after my appointment, but I sat there for a moment. I put my hands on my chest. I felt my heart and realized it was beating in a strong rhythm, but mostly, I noticed that my heart didn't feel broken anymore. It felt whole and loved, just like I felt whole and loved by myself and others.

When the time is right, I know I will meet someone special, but for now, I am happy and full of life. I had had a stroke of luck, and my newfound chance at life had given me a new view of everything.

When the time is right, I won't have to kiss frogs looking for a prince. When the time is right, I will meet a man, just a man that I can love, who will love me right back, and that's all that I will need—that and a way to tell Gianna that her persistence in wearing tacky eighties workout duds isn't really making a fabulous new fashion statement.

About the Author

Lia Rose is a teacher, a costume designer, a playwright, a Reiki master, and once starred in a zombie movie. She is the oldest of five children in an Italian family, and a mom of three adult sons from a rural town in central Connecticut. In her spare time, she enjoys writing, dancing, and all aspects of theater, most especially costume design and construction. Because humor is very important in her life, she also writes a blog called Meye2cents.com, which is her eye view of the funny world around her and also writes how-to blog called BeyondyourStage.com.

Lia Rose is also finishing work on a play, based on her book, called, "Kissing the Frogs!", which she hopes to have produced in 2018/2019.

CPSIA information can be obtained
at www.ICGtesting.com
Printed in the USA
LVHW09s1018240918
591165LV00002B/20/P

9 781642 144604